BEYOND
* * * * * THE * * * * *
MENU

BEYOND THE MENU

LAUNCHING AND MANAGING A PROFITABLE RESTAURANT

RAVI WAZIR

FOREWORD BY **AD SINGH**
PREFACE BY **GAURI DEVIDAYAL**

JAICO PUBLISHING HOUSE

Ahmedabad Bangalore Chennai
Delhi Hyderabad Kolkata Mumbai

Published by Jaico Publishing House
A-2 Jash Chambers, 7-A Sir Phirozshah Mehta Road
Fort, Mumbai - 400 001
jaicopub@jaicobooks.com
www.jaicobooks.com

BEYOND THE MENU
ISBN 978-81-19792-83-2

First Jaico Impression: 2024

Page design and layout by Inosoft Systems, Delhi

Contents

Section 4: Weathering Difficult Times

Foreword

Dear Reader,

Welcome to the industry I've made my world for over thirty years now. A few of us have been privileged to help shape and lead its growth over these years into the diverse, cool, and exciting space we are in today.

And the best part is that if we just look at trends and habits across Asia, there's still a huge opportunity for growth. The number of times people go out in a week will keep rising, as will the ratios of their spending on food against savings.

However, if you're looking to start your first restaurant, be warned that it is one of the most difficult enterprises for newcomers to succeed in. Worldwide.

It's particularly difficult in India, where we don't have industry status yet, nor is the ecosystem around us yet structured or helpful enough.

As such this book can be very valuable for you to help you take your first steps carefully and wisely.

I've known Ravi ever since he helmed the first Olive we

opened in Bombay in 2000, and it's from his experience and research he has created this book.

Take your time reading it and understanding it. Reach out to the National Restaurant Association of India (NRAI) or Ravi himself if you need further advice.

And then, get set to enjoy your own special magical journey. All the best.

—AD Singh
Managing Director, Olive Bar & Kitchen

Preface

Rewind to 2008, my husband Jay Yousuf, a computer engineer by education and a data communications entrepreneur in the US, had a crazy idea of opening a San Francisco inspired casual fine dining restaurant in Mumbai. I was in the thick of my career as a chartered accountant with a big four firm, and tried desperately to talk him out of it. Today, 16 years later, Jay and I are four restaurants, one bakery brand, one Indian cloud kitchen and one culinary event space deep in to the F&B world.

Opening a restaurant became part indulging our passion which was a love of creating a great dining experience, and part retirement plan. We've never worked harder in our lives and what began as one restaurant has grown into multiple operations. The thrill of getting a real-time satisfied reaction (for the most part) is addictive.

Today's Indian diner is exposed to and craving new concepts and new cuisines. The position of a chef has shifted from being a fallback career option to a sought after profession with potential celebrity status. However, equally important is the business of restaurants, the behind the scenes, the less glamourous aspect, which usually isn't managed by the same person wearing the creative hat.

Ravi's book addresses this crucial aspect of the business which often gets superseded in the name of passion and hope. I wish it had been around when I was getting started, but fortunately for you, it now is.

—**Gauri Devidayal**
Co-Founder, Food Matters Group,
and Author of *Diamonds for Breakfast*

Introduction

Over the years, whenever I have told people what I do for a living, at least one out of every ten has promptly shared that they would like to set up a restaurant of their own someday. A diverse range of individuals—corporate executives, homemakers, industrialists, landlords, celebrities, and even professional restaurant managers and chefs—seem to be interested in the restaurant business. Initially, I always wondered what led these varied people to share a common goal of setting up a restaurant. With several decades of experience in helping hospitality and food enterprises succeed, I now know why so many people nurture this desire.

However, before I share this interesting bit with you, let me walk you through how I got into this business in the first place. Thereon, let's begin with the basics of understanding what a restaurant really is, what it takes and how you can start one yourself.

A Walk Down Memory Lane

As a city-bred child, I often used to visit my paternal grandfather in the quaint town of Pahalgam, Kashmir, during my summer vacations. Beautiful horses, picturesque rivers, mountains, natural springs... the mere mention of Kashmir breathes life into these precious memories. However, one image that remains etched in my mind forever is that of my grandfather and his hotel.

Mount View Hotel, as it was known in the early 80s, was a favourite among the middle-class travellers back then. There were days when we faced challenges like the guests suddenly falling ill, or getting hurt by being too adventurous. And there were also days when some guests sought recommendations to visit local shops for buying traditional items, or enjoy local hospitality. No matter the nature of these experiences and challenges, my grandfather would always be there for his guests. The pride and sensitivity with which he cared for them was remarkable. This was my initiation into the hospitality and food business, and I realized very quickly then that this is what I'd like to do for a living.

My Early Influences in Food

It began at home. I was born to a Kashmiri Pandit father and a Parsi mother. Both sides of the family loved to plan their next meal, whilst eating their present one. So, thinking about food three to four times a day was perfectly normal for me. I grew up in Bandra, a diversely-populated suburb

(From left to right: The young, bespectacled author happily standing close to his grandfather, the hotelier, as his father watches him appreciatively with the author's younger brother to his side. The picture is captured in front of the Mount View Hotel, Srinagar.)

of Mumbai, and inhabited by Goans, Mangaloreans, East Indians, Bohris, Parsis, Hindus, and many such communities, on whose warm hospitality and delectable regional cuisines I was nurtured.

During my middle school years, I lived on the outskirts of Mysore near Brindavan Gardens, where my dad, an engineer, was transferred to look after a fertilizer factory. The diversity, flavour, and brilliance of the food there—involving South Indian cuisines from across Karnataka, Andhra, Tamil Nadu, and Coorg—astounded me. I feel fortunate to still stay connected with many of my friends and relatives from all over the country, with whom I shared several scrumptious meals, and many of their mothers fed me some of the most unforgettable dishes I have eaten till date.

I know that food means many things to many people, but at the core, for me, it has always been about emotion, gratitude, and a human connect.

What Is a Restaurant?

Now, let's understand what a restaurant is. A restaurant is typically a place where the public purchases meals or refreshments. The term 'restaurant' is believed to have been originated in Paris in 1765 thanks to a man named Mr. Boulanger who had first set up a soup kitchen. He had put up a sign on the door that allegedly read 'Boulanger débite des restaurants divins' (reportedly translated as 'Boulanger sells restoratives fit for the gods'). Over the years, entrées and main courses joined the menu, and the modern restaurant as we know it today, took shape.

As per the Mumbai municipality, a restaurant must have three sections: (i) A storage area for food and non-food items like packaging, (ii) a production area for cooking also known as the kitchen, and (iii) a service area known as the dining hall to serve food on the premises. How these three areas are built and maintained for their patrons tells us what kind of restaurant it is. For instance, if the cuisine is highly specialized with sophisticated service and ambience, then it is considered as a fine dining restaurant. If the food is prepared well in advance and served at a fast pace, then it is a quick-service or a fast-food restaurant. When a restaurant offers wide range of coffee and a space for casual conversations and friendly meet-ups, it is called a café. However, if an establishment has no dining area and simply a storage and production space which allows takeaways and food deliveries, then it is a cloud kitchen.

Like many ideas that have evolved over time to serve a larger purpose, the idea of a restaurant has now become an integral part of society. Restaurants have transformed into spaces of social networking, of discovering new cultures and cuisines from faraway lands, of spending an evening with your loved ones, of clinching business deals over a glass of wine, and so forth. All this, of course, in addition to its basic function of restoring people with the help of good food, good service, and good ambience—the three crucial pillars of a restaurant business.

Why Do People Want to Start Restaurants?

Every aspiring restaurateur has their own reason to start a restaurant.

- A corporate executive may want to escape the dreariness of a 9-to-5 job and have an idea for a restaurant worth launching.
- A landlord may have a space that he feels could be better monetized.
- A homemaker may be well-appreciated for their culinary skills and would want a wider platform.
- An industrialist may want a private venue to host their associates and friends.
- A celebrity may be looking to invest in a restaurant business.
- Restaurant managers or chefs may become tired of working for someone else and believe they can do a better job running their own business.

Are any of these the right reasons to start a restaurant?

Of course, they are! Let no one tell you otherwise. Whether you want to start a restaurant as an escape, to socialize, to earn more money, to earn fame, or to find a creative platform for your culinary skills, it is the right reason... for you.

To run a successful restaurant, however, you will need to take the time to understand the business holistically, to recognize what you bring to the table, what you don't, and figure out a way to bridge that gap... by bringing in what you lack.

What Does It Take?

Notoriously, one in every three restaurants doesn't survive its first year of existence. Considering that for an eatery to survive anywhere in the world for even three years is an accomplishment, one that survives and thrives for a decade or more and across generations is nothing short of legendary. When speaking in hushed tones about successful eateries, even the most indifferent of audiences speculate with enthusiasm about the sacks full of money that owners must be taking home and the secret ingredients that they must be using to get their guests addicted.

Considering the significant amount of speculation that has existed on successful eateries since forever, and even more so post-pandemic, credible insights will be a refreshing change. This book will lead audiences to truly understand what it takes to build and sustain a restaurant brand with such longevity. At a simplistic level, all it takes is a good idea fuelled by a good location, good people, and good food, packaged in a good marketing plan, but not without an eye on the finances. Money is the oxygen of a business and without it, you can't fuel your passion. There's an industry joke: In the restaurant business, it takes a large fortune to make a small one. There is a good amount of truth to this. Besides these elements, there are many more one should consider to be a successful restaurateur, and getting it all right isn't easy, even for the most experienced ones. We have all heard of instances when experienced restaurateurs have failed and people with no experience in the industry succeeded.

So, deep down, we know that the restaurateur's industry experience doesn't necessarily matter. What truly matters for a restaurant's success is the restaurateur's willingness and ability to prioritize certain tasks and attitudes over others. This is what we will discover throughout the course of this book.

As students of the restaurant business, we must fundamentally build our understanding of two things—how a restaurant works and how entrepreneurship works. This guide accomplishes just that. Your thoughts will change each day as you keep sharpening your plan. Therefore, putting it down on paper and tweaking it as you go is the best way to capture your concept. Setting timelines for both your short-term and long-term goals, and being nimble in improvising, serve the needs and wants of your audience.

Managing relationships is the toughest and most crucial part of the restaurant business, which is why it is sometimes referred to as 'the people business'. Looking after 'people' here doesn't only involve your guests and staff members, but also the neighbouring community, licensing authorities, and the media. It is extremely crucial to put yourself in your customer's shoes when making decisions about food, service, ambience, and, most importantly, pricing and portion sizes. Even the wealthiest of consumers expect good value for their money. A restaurant that consistently delivers in all these areas and meets or exceeds customer expectations undoubtedly tips the odds in its favour.

Keep in mind that not every restaurant that succeeds delivers excellence on all fronts from the day it opens. However, it is important to do well enough on most fronts so that the customers will be willing to forgive your early mistakes, allowing your business to survive. If you can demonstrate that you truly listen, promptly act upon their complaints, and often even consider their suggestions, the marketplace will reward you with a deep sense of pride and achievement that only a restaurateur can experience.

So, onward we go with our goal towards understanding the restaurant business. It is a mistake, however, to underestimate the emotional wherewithal one needs to succeed. As American celebrity chef and author Anthony Bourdain once famously said, "If anything is good for pounding humility into you permanently, it's the restaurant business."

Since I graduated from the Institute of Hotel Management, Mumbai, in 1988, I have had the privilege of being in a front row seat in the decision-making and problem-solving processes of many restaurants and other food businesses during their start-up and growth years.

The four sections in this book—The Vision Board, Going Live, Running Your Restaurant, and Weathering Difficult Times—can come in handy and accompany you in your journey of understanding the restaurant business. This book—based on decades of experience in the hospitality industry, studying both the successes and failures—is intended to serve as your roadmap for the restaurant business to assuage the financial and emotional pain of aspiring restaurateurs.

As with all businesses, an idea, only when accompanied by an action, gives birth to a restaurant. Procrastination and fear, the worst enemies of action, can best be conquered by gaining a deeper understanding of the subject through good research and coming to terms with its challenges through self-conviction.

This book will walk you through that process. The rest is up to you!

- - - - - -

Note: Some sections of the book, for example, Licensing and Permissions may be specific to Mumbai (India). International readers and those from other states will need to research and comply with the government regulations applicable to their area.

The currency used throughout is the Indian Rupee (INR). US $1 is approximately ₹83 as of January 2024. Of course, simply converting the amount may be inappropriate at times since the value of various goods and services varies widely from country to country.

If you come across a word you don't recognize, you can look it up in the 'Glossary' at the end of the book.

Section I

The Vision Board

To be able to build something, you must first **see** it in your mind's eye, then **prepare** to understand what it entails, and finally, make a **plan**.

Only after preparing a solid vision board can you make an informed decision on whether your business can be operational.

How to 'See' the Restaurant Business

Similar to the human body, which has lifelines such as the circulatory and respiratory systems, as well as vital organs like the heart and lungs, I perceive a restaurant business as a living entity with its own lifelines and constituent parts.

I have found the following visualisation model useful in gauging the pulse of all kinds of food businesses regardless of their lifecycles.

Imagine a plain white cardboard shoe box. Now, remove its lid, and you will see that it has walls and a floor. Can you visualize it from above? Let's resize this box a little larger than it presently is—maybe the size of a doll house.

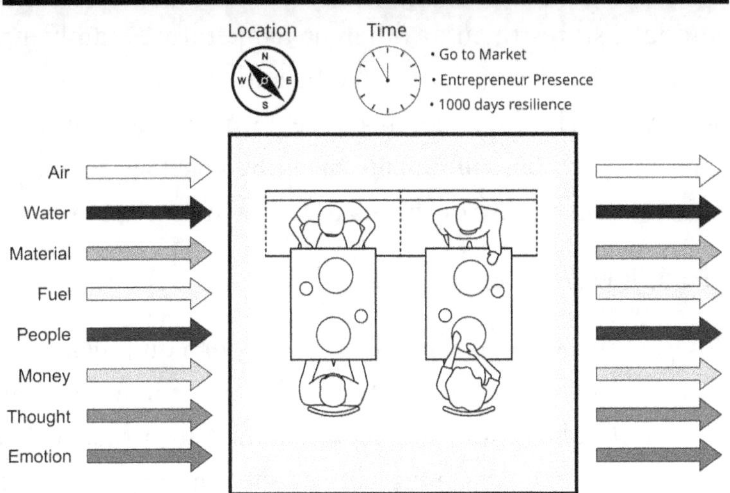

We can imagine different rooms inside, for instance, the stores, kitchen, dining area, etc.

Now, within this space, let's visualize eight different pipelines (or lifelines) entering and exiting this box, along with two additional parts. So, imagine...

1. Air-flow (White):

Imagine a white duct bringing in fresh outside air into this white room and removing stale, hot air, to ensure the comfort of both your guests in the dining area and your staff in the kitchen.

2. Water-flow (Blue):

Next, we have a blue pipeline bringing in fresh water for drinking, cooking, and cleaning, through taps at basins, while the dirty water flows out from the drains below.

3. Material-flow (Orange):

Visualize a broad orange pipeline that brings in raw food materials, stores them at different temperatures (ambient, refrigerated, frozen, and cooked), and disposes of waste food. Similarly, imagine this pipe bringing in non-food materials such as equipment, furniture, packaging items, etc., and dispatching or disposing of them as necessary.

4. Fuel-flow (Yellow):

Now, to run our business space and our equipment, we need electricity, gas, and other fuels. So, imagine yellow lines of electricity and gas pipes running into this room. Remember, this flow must be uninterrupted, safe, and efficient.

5. People-flow (Brown):

The food business is actually a people business. To convert our vision to reality, we require guests, staff, vendors, etc. Occasionally, we also need partners to help us with time, money, and skills that we may not have. So, just imagine outside the box: guests parking their cars and walking into your restaurant, being seated; vendors bringing in supplies from the service entrance, and staff managing the operation, both in the kitchen and the dining area. Remember, it will take some good marketing to get these people in. Speaking of people, don't forget that our neighbours, licensing authorities, and reviewers are also stakeholders outside our box, and play a significant role in our success or failure.

6. Money-flow (Green):

As I mentioned earlier, without money our business cannot survive. The equipment, food, and people that we have just visualized in our space is only possible with money. Visualize money flowing into your restaurant through green pipelines as capital. Even if it's a loan, imagine it flowing out with its principal and interest. Also, envision money flowing in continuously from our guests as they pay, filling in your cash drawers and bank accounts. Similarly, picture money flowing out for the rent, utilities, salaries, and food each month.

7. Thought-flow (Purple):

Our very first step when we start this business is to think. It begins with an idea that we develop into a concept. Some of these thoughts, which flow through the purple pipeline, will be our own, while others will be brought into our enterprise by individuals or partners we collaborate with or hire. The work culture of our company, the agility of our decision-making, and problem-solving approach, all reflect our flow of thoughts within this box. Imagine thoughts related to our value proposition flowing outside this box in the form of communication to our guests.

8. Emotion-flow (Red):

Now, imagine passion flowing into your business, bringing with it a great positive energy that is contagious and spreading it on to others in your business. Visualize the personal issues each person may be facing and the resilience with which they continue to smile through them. Picture each person in the box smiling and working with sincerity.

These eight pipes or flows in the business are its lifelines. Opening and closing these flow taps to the right extent and for the right duration that benefits the business can either make or break your business.

To complete the picture, add just two more parts. Visualize the box again. Where is your restaurant located?

9. Location:

Rather where should it be located? Let's place it where our target audience can best access it. Or, if it's a cloud kitchen, place it near a market where raw materials can easily be sourced or in spaces where your consumers have prompt access to order food service. It's crucial to check how affordable the space is or can be and if it has an appropriate licence.

The last thing to remember is the importance of...

10. Time:

- Is the concept correctly timed in the market place? Is it relevant?
- Is the entrepreneur investing sufficient time to their business, especially during its nascent stage or when the business is performing poorly?
- Is the entrepreneur committed to dedicating 1,000 days to the business to give it a fair chance in the marketplace?

I, therefore, believe that visualizing the restaurant business using these ten steps will help you map and control nearly everything that can be mapped and controlled within it.

- When I plan to open a new restaurant, this is how I see it.
- When I study operations of a restaurant to grow its business, this is how I see it.
- When I diagnose and resolve problems of an existing restaurant, this is how I see it.

Now, I hope that this is how you will see it too.

How to Prepare

The preparation stage requires your attention in two areas—the restaurant and the business.

The Restaurant

Starting a restaurant takes tremendous effort, patience, and strength—both physical and mental. It requires in-depth planning and a focused effort, while constantly networking with the agencies involved. Outlining crucial work objectives from the start works well. For instance, it's important to chart out the type of restaurant you plan to open, its main objectives, the concept, how you will analyze and penetrate the market, capital required, financial projections, and the tentative operational structure.

Let's not forget, time and money are prime considerations. Once you invest the money, the sooner you get the restaurant started, the better. However, starting without adequate preparations is a sure formula for failure. You need to push for completion without ignoring the smallest detail. For this reason, it certainly helps to know exactly what you want, and how to go about it. Of course, market changes will still require constant improvisation of the original plan, and this flexibility must be a part of your planning. During the pandemic, we learnt that predicting all eventualities is impossible. All we can do is be better prepared by running a lean operation and squirreling away some savings.

There will be implications on various personal areas of life, including work hours, health, family, as well as financial and psychological considerations. Sleepless nights, obnoxious customers, legal hassles, and financial problems are common teething troubles everyone goes through, and some of these are a recurring feature. You will need to factor all these into your preparation.

Broadly, the areas you need to look into include:

Finances

You need to consider your ability to raise capital, either from your own funds, through loans, or from other investors. The initial investment required may be in terms of down payment, instalments, reserves, or working capital. Make sure not to embark on a project where expenses might exceed your capacity. Many restaurants that start without a well-detailed financial plan end up either being aborted or sold out for equity.

Resource management

It is crucial for a restaurateur to first define the kind of resources required to deliver the brand promise to the patrons in terms of people, materials, machines, money, and, most importantly, the time frame within which such resources can be deployed. It is best to be clear about which of these activities you will handle personally and which ones you may delegate or outsource, and to what extent.

Location

A new location involves practical considerations such as availability of the venue, visibility and accessibility, presence of competitors, required size of premises, licensing hurdles, parking availability, and neighbourhood relationships.

It may be wiser to take up an existing restaurant which has already acquired mandatory licenses and permissions. Some neighbourhoods may be opposed to the idea of a restaurant in their locality on account of the probable public nuisance. The disadvantage of such a location is the difficulty of changing the public perception attached to the earlier operation.

Market analysis and penetration

This has to be detailed so as to accurately position and price the product, which is critical for the restaurant's success. Additionally, publicity, promotional plans, marketing, advertising, and other such aspects also need to be defined clearly.

Concept

The ambience of the place essentially determines the kind of clientele the restaurant will attract. It is therefore advisable to invest in a good architect and designer who can create a space with a preferred theme.

Licensing and permissions

This can be the most exasperating of all your entrepreneurial tasks. Various governmental departments need to be contacted for approvals in order to run your restaurant. For instance, a number of licenses need to be procured, including food selling license, health department clearance, building permissions, fire brigade clearance, company registration, trade mark (logo) application, Employee State Insurance Scheme (ESIS), structural slab certificate, police clearance, garbage clearance, music playing license, excise licenses, etc.

Remember, the departments concerned in each state of our country have their own rules and fees for issuing relevant licenses, which are subject to constant change. In Mumbai, for instance, the Brihanmumbai Municipal Corporation (BMC) handed me a checklist of documents to be submitted to their health department in order to obtain a health license. You will be able to find this list on their official website. This is the first step towards the long, gruelling journey of procuring other mandatory licenses for your restaurant. While submitting restaurant applications in Mumbai can now be done online, one still has to visit various departments in person often for a follow-up. Once you get a go-ahead from the health department, you need to seek permission from other agencies such as the fire brigade, local police, excise department (for liquor), etc. It would be wise to figure out whether the municipal office of your city can provide you with such a list as it may come in handy.

Licenses often have a rationale to them. For instance, a restaurant to have an exit or a second door is often a compulsory demand of the fire department as an escape route for guests or staff in the event of a fire. To give you another example: there are strict rules against playing loud music in case of an event after 10 p.m. in any locality in Mumbai; you need a mandatory 'Loudspeaker Permission' from the BMC before hosting such an event. This is meant to avoid disturbance to the neighbourhood.

On some occasions, however, rules are vague and even conflicting. For instance, a rule from one government department may require you to close your restaurant by 1:30 a.m., while another department may generously allow you to run your restaurant 24/7. This leads to misunderstandings and conflicts between restaurateurs and the said departments. Hotel and restaurant associations may provide some clarity or help in such cases, however, even they have their limitations and can only support you up to a point.

Preparing and dealing with the bureaucracy in restaurant industry includes an excruciatingly long wait and, sometimes, even greasing the wheels. Retaining the services of an agent is therefore advisable to overcome this hurdle with the least possible investment of time, finances, and headache. A single-window system that addresses all the requisite permissions and reduces the bureaucratic obstacles, sadly, still remains a dream.

Some licenses and permissions required in Mumbai

Company Registration: For basic creation of a legal entity, with the help of a Chartered Accountant.

Trademark Registration: For clearance to use the Company Name (to be eventually copyrighted), with the help of a Chartered Accountant.

Sales Tax Registration: To file monthly returns via the Sales Tax Department.

Shops and Establishments Registration: For the registration certificate of establishment of the business, via the Shops and Establishments Inspector at the municipal ward office.

Fire Department Clearance: For clearance of following fire safety norms, via the Chief Fire Officer.

Water Connection Certificate: For obtaining water connection based on the grade of the restaurant, via the Water Department of the relevant municipal ward office.

Health License: For food and liquor service, via the Health Department at the relevant municipal ward office.

Police Registration Certificate (P.P.E.E.): For obtaining a sanction for a place of public gathering, via the Office of the Commissioner / Asst. Commissioner of Police (local station).

Gradation Certificate: For Grades I, II or III based infrastructure, sanitary conditions, and medical examination of staff, via the Health Department at the municipal ward office.

Receipts of Trade Refuse Charges: For garbage clearance, via the Health Department at the municipal ward office.

Public Performance License: For authorization to play sound or recorded music, via Phonographic Performance Limited.

Pollution Clearance: For clearance of pollution safety norms, via the City Engineer (Civil) at the Environment Department.

Structural Slab Certificate: For certification of the strength of the structure after renovation via an engineer authorized by the relevant municipal ward office.

Board License: For temporary shed construction or roof extension during monsoons via the Building License Department at the municipal ward office.

ESIS (Employee State Insurance Scheme): For shops and establishments employing more than ten staff members, via a labour law consultant.

State Excise and Prohibition License: For a Permit Room (to serve liquor), via the Excise Department.

Food and Drug Control Act License (F.D.A.): For prevention of adulteration of food and beverage, via the State Health Ministry.

FSSAI: For adherence of all food safety norms, via the FSSAI.

Health Certificate for kitchen staff: For ascertaining if staff carry any infectious diseases that can be passed on to consumers, via the Health Department doctor at the municipal ward office.

Neon/Glow-sign License: For advertising fees, via the License Department at the municipal ward office.

> **Weights and Measurements Certificate:** For verification of weighing scales used on the premises, via the State Weights and Measurement Department.
>
> **Excise Account Register:** For maintaining records pertaining to the sale of liquor, via the Excise Department.

Agreements

Stable relationships with crucial people in the business such as landlords and partners develop over time. However, people have the tendency to change, their attitudes may evolve, and they may even forget the subtle nuances of the arrangement that were once agreed upon. In order to bridge this gap that may possibly occur in future, regardless of how well or how long you know the person in question, it is best to legally document all the points that were agreed upon. Involving a lawyer for the drafting of the official agreements and contracts, deciding on the value of stamp paper, etc., is advisable.

Layout

A stand-alone or an independent restaurant does not enjoy the same support facilities—like the one we see in a hotel—such as an office, staff dining area, extra storage space, etc. So, besides trying to accommodate the maximum number of seats (without overcrowding your guests), it is important to have good space allocation for 'back of the house' areas like the kitchen (pre-preparation and preparation), storage area (cold, dry, and liquor stores), staff facilities (dining area, lockers, and toilets), pot-wash and office space. These elements form the backbone of the operation, and without a strong spine, the business can't deliver.

You could apportion the space within the restaurant based on:

- The type of service (dine-in, take-away, etc.)
- The kind of cuisine (regional, fine dining, pizzeria, etc.)
- The number of patrons expected to be served.

For example, at a dine-in regional-cuisine restaurant, some rules of thumb are:

- Dining area to back-of-the-house operations ratio is 60:40
- Dining hall area is generally eight to twenty square feet per cover. (The more luxurious your offering, the more the elbow room.)
- Back-end space break-up (an example):
  Kitchen: 50%, Stores: 20%, Pot-wash: 15%, Staff area: 10%, Office: 5%

Obviously exceptions to the rule would be based on space constraints and the need for optimum utilization of high-street space for revenue generation. Renting nearby premises at a lower rate per sq. ft. for auxiliary facilities that are not necessarily required on-site (such as an office), will address this issue.

Professional services

It is often necessary to identify and retain the services of professional agencies, including an accountant, an architect and interior designer, a civil engineer, a kitchen layout consultant, licensing agents, an attorney, a recruitment consultant, security services, a PR and event management firm, etc.

Major systems

Water, electricity, gas, exhaust, air-conditioning, and computer systems are critical to the operation, and a balance between quality and expense needs to be maintained.

Banking

Identify a nearby bank with suitable facilities. Your capital investment and cash/credit-card receipts should pass through your main bank account. The manager may be provided with a weekly or bi-weekly 'float' for minor daily expenses. A petty cash account can be set up for these transactions. Savings accounts set-up for staff in the same bank will facilitate easy salary payment online each month. Signatories for the bank account should be decided based on their reliability and availability.

Equipment required

- Kitchen equipment – stoves, utensils, refrigerators, mixers, ovens, etc.
- Telephones
- Water purifier and cooler
- Exhaust system

- Furniture and fixtures – tables, chairs, side stations, artefacts, etc.
- Service equipment – cutlery, crockery, glassware, table appointments, other service-ware, etc.
- Stores equipment – weighing scale, shelving, storage racks, cabinets, freezers, etc.
- Maintenance equipment – vacuum cleaner, smoke gun (for mosquitoes), sand buckets, fire extinguishers, etc.
- Staff uniforms and lockers
- Toilet accessories – hand driers, soap dispensers, tissue papers, toilet cleaners, etc.
- Cashier's cabin – Credit card machine, safe, drawers, etc.
- Air-conditioning
- Computers and other tech such as hand-held order-taking devices
- Vehicles for deliveries or purchases
- Soft drink gun and cylinders, beer taps, and canisters

The selection of equipment may be based on specific requirements like the cost, supplier reliability, space constraints, after sales service, etc. Don't forget to consider cost effectiveness of any equipment by measuring its lifespan/depreciation, and fuel consumption—say, gas vs. electricity.

A few must-have systems

- Accounting–receipts (for billing), payments (credit and salaries), Profit and Loss, etc.

- Inventory and Purchase systems
- Housekeeping and Property Management
- Management Information Systems
- Guest Reservations and order-taking machines
- Excise Book for liquor
- Communication systems (online and offline), including website, social media platforms, public relations through bloggers, news publications, etc.

While the above systems are best supported through effective software, a manual backup (wherever possible), must also be provided.

Becoming a member of restaurant associations such as the National Restaurant Association of India (NRAI), the Federation of Hotel & Restaurant Associations of India (FHRAI), or Indian Hotel & Restaurant Association (AHAR), has its advantages. They provide updates on the latest government policies, a bit of support while liaising with the government and other relevant bodies, offer updates on new policies, have a WhatsApp group that might be of help in recruitment, and provide information on numerous other areas of the market and the hospitality industry.

Managing restaurant operations is mainly common sense. It is best to stick to the basics. Setting standard operating procedures while allowing a good degree of flexibility, will go a long way in helping you achieve your goals.

The Business

"It is not because things are difficult that we do not dare, it is because we do not dare that things are difficult." – Seneca

Having transitioned from being an employee to becoming an entrepreneur, and having helped many others follow suit, I discovered that one of the greatest differences between the two is that of mindset. Apart from letting go of a steady income through employment, the unpredictable nature of working hours and the uncertainty which comes with running a business, makes it rather challenging to manage your daily expenses and a desired lifestyle with every passing day.

One entrepreneur I worked with found it tough to let go of his job as a senior executive at a large multinational firm as he began prepping for his start-up. He asked me to manage the operations of his start-up during the initial stages while he stayed employed, and so I did. However, he also wanted me to launch the restaurant in his absence. Although I gladly agreed, I suggested that he back his substantial financial investment with his personal presence and complete focus. If—for some reason and despite my most sincere efforts—the business failed, he would never forgive himself. Following my suggestion, he left his job half-heartedly and after some initial success, was unable to sustain it and had to shut down his business.

If you are making such a move, from being an employee to becoming an entrepreneur, try and surround yourself with all types of entrepreneurs for inspiration and motivation. This may even lead you to one of those rare times when a piece of advice from a small scrappy idli vendor on a bicycle might be of greater value than that of a senior business leader of a large food company.

The word 'entrepreneur' comes from the French verb 'entreprendre' meaning 'to undertake', in reference to Frenchmen who organized and led military expeditions. Today, it refers to a person who organizes, operates, and assumes the risk for a business venture.

> "A reluctant entrepreneur sets himself up for failure."

Entrepreneurs appear to be an elusive group of people who inevitably generate interest and evoke strong reactions. Some who have made it big on sheer grit are admired while others who have allegedly made it with influence or luck are scorned. Either way they can rarely be ignored. Whether out of mere curiosity or a genuine need to understand this enigmatic breed, everyone wants to know what it takes to be a successful entrepreneur, particularly if one is not born into an entrepreneurial family or the one that is wealthy.

If we look at entrepreneurs around us, we see that their backgrounds may be rich or poor, their education from a renowned institution or off the street, their age group young or old, their attitude humble or arrogant, their motivation the identification of a market gap or the pressure of circumstance, their style subdued or flamboyant. So, there is no stereotypical personality of an entrepreneur that we can blindly copy and become successful.

How, then, can we go about capturing the essence of this mystery of being a successful entrepreneur in brief? Since the distinguishing factor of entrepreneurs are their thoughts and actions, the answer to the question lies in analyzing this factor and determining if there is a recurring pattern.

Over the years, I have worked under several talented entrepreneurs and been fortunate to study their styles and methods at close quarters. I have also experienced the start-up and failure of my own business. Reading numerous business case studies and biographies of great entrepreneurs have further assisted me in presenting some of the findings I'm about to share. At the end of this reading however, you will have to draw your own conclusions.

While some entrepreneurs are born into an entrepreneurial family, there are many who have made it on their own—people who have either no business background or are self-taught. So, entrepreneurship is something that can be learnt. It generally involves shifting economic resources from an area of lower yield to one of higher yield. This necessitates two crucial abilities:

a) **A Resource-Focused Ability** that involves availing opportunities in the lower yield area. Resources refer to money, machines, materials, labour, and time.

b) **A Challenge-Seeking Ability** that involves identifying opportunities in the higher yield area.

Based on this concept, the following grid attempts to capture the types of entrepreneurs that exist:

Resource-Focused vs. Challenge-Seeking

		Resource-Focused Approach	
		Low	High
Challenge - Seeking Approach	High	**Gambling Entrepreneur** Grabs opportunities with little thought to the resource consequences of his actions. Seems to survive but eventually fails at the end of the start-up period.	**Rich Entrepreneur** He displays a high degree of ability in both areas and balances risks, resources, and rewards though a process of periodic review. He is a risk manager rather than a risk taker, in that he does his homework well and limits his financial exposure. For example, he may relinquish even the best client contracts if they seem doubtful on the cash receivable front. This is the most successful type—one that we'd obviously like to study.
	Low	**Non Entrepreneur** Low in both challenge-seeking as well as resource-focus areas, they land up opting for "me too" businesses that inevitably fail.	**Incomplete Entrepreneur** Too resource-focused to actualize business opportunities that come his way. Generally, attributes failure to lack of resources. While his caution prevents failure it also doesn't allow the business to grow. At best he manages to survive.

This grid has been derived from Rajan Chhibba's book *Starting A Successful Business: A Step-by-Step Guide*. This model of classifying entrepreneurship on the basis of just two dimensions is rather simplistic, but it does offer some sort of a framework for understanding the concept.

Some ways entrepreneurs think

- Businessmen don't just create thought, but apply it and find a practical path to implementing their idea. Hiring the right person for each role, allowing them to do their job, and supporting them through it, is a great example of this.
- Regardless of the naysayers, entrepreneurs are driven enough to follow their dreams. It is important to be watchful of who is telling you what, how skilled they are in that area, and what their agenda is.
- Entrepreneurs recognize the difference between an idea and an opportunity. An opportunity is an idea that the market wants and is willing to pay for. One of the many cases in which this is visible, is when restaurants (across the world), which only served lunch and dinner, began opening up with a breakfast menu as well, thereby hugely improving the monetization of this whole new meal time with existing infrastructure.
- Entrepreneurs can see possibilities in situations where others see none, and have the patience to work out a solution despite variables out of their control.
- They ask themselves the right questions. Basically, the what, why, when, and how of starting the

business they have in mind. For example, during market studies they may not purely depend on existing research-based reports, but will also do their own primary investigation and research since they recognize that strong input data leads to more accurate conclusions.

- They consider their tolerance for risk versus their desire for reward. Rather than complain about the lack of something, they make up for it with extra effort.
- They believe that neither experience nor education can ensure success in business. What matters, is what you do with opportunities.
- The approach is one of ownership—taking responsibility for failure—and being unafraid to think differently from the herd.
- They have curiosity, gather knowledge and skills to constantly modify their approach, perspective, and behaviour to improve their business performance. Possessing the mindset of a student and a steward of one's business helps its growth.
- Entrepreneurs know that their success depends on the acceptance of their offering in the marketplace. So, they embrace change and respond with flexibility. The most obvious one being, genuinely listening to your guests and team for improved alignment with your patrons' needs.
- They recognize that good time-management (at least to the extent that they can control) is critical since delays equal to a huge waste of resources. Prioritizing

tasks on a to-do list is an example of how to focus time as a resource.

- Entrepreneurs look at the big picture as well the day-to-day activities. They do the right things and also endeavour to do things right.

- An unshakeable belief in oneself and one's ideas, supported by the ability to bounce back, is absolutely necessary to overcome uncertainties. Restaurateurs, whose restaurants survived the pandemic, had the spirit and courage to take each day as it comes. Though in all fairness, not every restaurateur with great self-belief was able to overcome pandemic-induced challenges safely.

- Entrepreneurs without any industry background familiarize themselves with the sector concerned to an extent that is equal to or greater than that of people from the sector.

- While they hire people with skills in finance, marketing, human resources, and/or operations, they also develop their own knowledge in these areas. For example, not every restaurant owner knows how to cook or even likes to cook.

- An executive seeks compensation and nurturing, typically working with defined duties and responsibilities. An entrepreneur seeks rewards and self-actualization, doing whatever it takes.

Some ways entrepreneurs act

- The energy, intensity, and stamina of an entrepreneur is fuelled by such love that constraints like age or health become irrelevant. For instance, Colonel Sanders of KFC and Ray Kroc of McDonald's began their journey with these brands in their middle age.

- They commit themselves to action and love the journey rather than the destination. This does not mean ignoring the short-term impacts that they naturally stay watchful of.

- They are great relationship managers, for the sake of their business. Even introverts work on this area and rise above their natural inclination to do what it takes to serve the business.

- They focus on their goals and timelines using cross-check mechanisms to keep track. For example, studying a food cost control sheet at the end of each month.

- Having the stomach to contain fear and step out of one's comfort zone, while taking a well-considered risk is the hallmark of a successful entrepreneur. For example, diligently learning and practising aspects of the business that they may be totally unfamiliar with, or find mundane.

- Entrepreneurs with long-term goals, work inch by inch to build their reputation by honouring their word. Others have a short-term perspective.

- They are careful with their money and don't waste capital regardless of whether it is their own or borrowed funds. For instance, simple saving techniques—from switching off electrical equipment when not in use, choosing cheaper forms of travel, etc.,—come in handy.

Whether or not all of the above thoughts and actions can be learned or are even necessary for entrepreneurial success is debatable. The fact is that everyone possesses some or many of these qualities to a varying degree, and can practise and/or enhance them while developing their unique success style.

In a sense, everyone is an entrepreneur. In an employer-employee relationship, for instance, you are in fact selling your time and expertise to a single client, i.e., your employer. One Harvard professor went so far as to say that pursuing entrepreneurship is actually safer, since you have multiple clients in a business as opposed to just one 'client' in a job.

How does one define success in a restaurant business? Udupi restaurant owners believe a thousand days is a good time frame to decide on the viability of the business.

You may evaluate this using these three criteria:

1. At least 40% of your client base is that of repeat customers.
2. You have begun ploughing your surplus cash back into your business towards asset building, such as real estate, equipment, training, etc. During the pandemic, we saw that most restaurateurs had not done this and were badly cash-strapped.
3. You have commenced using your business cash surplus towards personal wealth creation through investments.

Before taking the plunge, ask yourself if you have the following in terms of willingness and abilities:

1. To operate and make decisions while shouldering all the responsibilities for the business.
2. To work hard and make necessary sacrifices.
3. Self-confidence and discipline to build the new business and persevere till you succeed.

Talking to successful entrepreneurs, getting some of them to become your mentor (someone who can bring about favourable changes in your thinking and behaviour), and reading some biographies of entrepreneurs can also be inspiring.

If you are looking for immediate results, think about these words by Ray Kroc: "People are always amazed by the fact that I didn't start McDonald's before I was 52 years old, and that I was an overnight success. But I was just like so many people in the entertainment business who practice their routine for years with hardly any notice, and then suddenly find themselves in the spotlight to stardom. I did achieve success from one day to the next, that's true, but my 30 years of preparation were like a long, long night!"

These thoughts and actions are meant to motivate you, but eventually it is you who needs to enlist your own targeted developmental areas and work on them. If you believe you have it all already, what are you waiting for? Let's move on to the next step. After all, as they say–footprints on the sands of time are not made by sitting down.

Now, let's look at the specifics on designing your restaurant, managing it as a project, and handling its cash flow and funding.

How to Design Your Restaurant

If you are imagining, why not imagine the best scenario? Imagine your restaurant guests as not just visitors, but as raving fans who endorse your brand and protect it with a certain degree of possessiveness. Now, what does that take?

Here are a few examples of what I have seen legendary restaurants practise:

> **"To build something that lasts, start with the end game in mind!"**

- They create one or more 'never-before' dishes or styles of presentation or service that challenge the thinking of their patrons.
- They empower their team at all levels to listen to and respond with openness to any negative feedback of their patrons.
- They take objective business decisions, especially when something or someone is hurting their business.
- They build a system that double-checks appearance, taste, etc., of every dish before it is served.

Either way, legendary restaurants—like legendary people—become so by standing taller than the rest. They become famous not just by doing great things, but by doing them repeatedly. Fans consider repeated excellence important, since delivering excellence once or even a few times might simply be considered good luck. Consistent excellence, however, can only be borne out of consistent deliberate effort. Therefore, people conclude that the brand behind it must be extraordinary and should be acknowledged as such.

"To be successful you have to be selfish, or else you will never achieve. And once you get to your highest level, then you have to be unselfish. Stay reachable. Stay in touch. Don't isolate."
— Michael Jordan.

Designing a restaurant space requires attention to aesthetics and functionality. After all, apart from how it looks, it is the efficient flow of people, materials, infrastructure, etc., within the restaurant that determines how well it works.

Capturing your vision in brick and mortar requires a bent of mind that is cued in to trends, possesses an understanding of the day-to-day operations and the psychographics of your target audience. These nuances must be considered from the perception of both your patrons as well as your operating staff for your design to be effective.

Aesthetics

When it comes to aesthetics, each person has their unique sensibility. What appeals to one may repel others. When creating a certain mood for a particular restaurant, it is patrons' sensibility that must be kept in mind.

Colours, textures, sounds, elbow room, and even aromas influence the patron's receptivity towards your space and your brand. Leverage each of these five senses.

The promoter of a national coffee shop chain once rightly pointed out to me how coffee shops were becoming so generic in their design, that one could hardly differentiate between them once you walked past the sign at the entrance. A good restaurant design extends through all the elements across its space, from the crockery to the menu card, from the uniforms to the toilet. Every element whether well-thought through or not, speaks to your patron.

Lighting contributes immensely to the mood of a space. Adjusting it at various hours of the day and night can alter the level of cheer, cosiness, and even the energy level amongst the guests and staff.

The sound of a sizzler being transported through a restaurant inevitably generates interest. One musically-inclined restaurateur friend of mine wisely began investing in better sound systems than the average restaurateur did at that time. His agenda was to enhance his guest experience through the often neglected sense of sound. He taught me that a sound system is only as good as the acoustics of the space within which it functions. His detailed planning of what music to play at which time of the day paid good dividends.

Certain smells can favourably influence us in certain spaces. The aroma of freshly-ground coffee beans in a coffee shop, or the scent of an orange in a juice bar convey purity and authenticity. It is interesting to note that such subconscious signals can be orchestrated within the human mind by injecting doses of certain fragrances into the space at regular intervals. Aromatizers, which house chemical-based scents rather than the real thing, achieve this objective surprisingly well.

Textures such as ruggedly finished log tables at an all-male bar, or smoothly surfaced ones at a child-friendly restaurant reflect the attitude of the restaurant towards its target audience.

Colours also affect the mood and behaviour of the patrons. Some colours are considered lucky and others trendy; some evoke certain emotions, and others, certain expectations.

Gaining an understanding of all these sensory aspects and applying them to your own concept will help you consistently deliver your brand promise and also engage, attract, and retain your patrons.

Functionality

How you envision the movement of people and materials within your restaurant will help you decide the various aspects of its layout.

Specialists in Heating, Ventilation, and Air Conditioning (HVAC), kitchen, and bar design, etc., must provide detailed inputs to the architect for incorporation into his master layout so as to avoid operational issues at a later stage. After all, the architect is involved in the project only as long as it is a 'site', and hands it over to the operational team once it's ready to be run as a restaurant.

Space allocation within the restaurant is also very much a part of design. Not just how to apportion the revenue area, the bar, the kitchen, and the stores, but also the sub-allocation of each area. For instance, if we look at storage space, we may divide it into food and non-food areas. Further, within the food storage areas, we need to subdivide it into foods stored at varying temperatures—ambient, refrigerated, and frozen. In order to arrive at how much storage space each of these areas need, you will have to decide: (a) the number of days you need to stock each of these three types of foods and, (b) how much space you will require to store each of them based on estimated sales. This is complicated, and requires guesstimated assumptions, but can be done and will hold you in good stead if you have good people and adequate planning time.

Even the best conceived restaurant designs in the world mean nothing without a relentless attention to execution. Proper execution in restaurant design invariably means effective project management.

Project Management

Managing start-up design

Time and money are crucial to a restaurant's capital costs, and even to its survival during the initial project stage. I have often seen overruns in time and money during the nascent stages of business start-ups. They invariably result in painful consequences.

On one occasion, an entrepreneur had to scale down their vision to a level which cannot possibly earn the originally projected return on investment; and in another instance, a situation had forced the entrepreneur to dilute their own equity in the business. Bearing these difficulties in mind, it is best to aggressively monitor and control the time and money you spend on your start-up.

Of all your restaurant start-up tasks, your architect and civil contractor invariably control the one with the longest duration. The largest part of your overall restaurant budget often comes under the scope of these two service providers. Once they are onboard, you are pretty much locked in with them, so it's best to continually monitor actual schedules and costs versus those projected. This has a significant impact on the outcome of your project. Thus, it will serve you well to:

a) Thoroughly investigate their depth of knowledge and integrity beforehand.
b) Agree and close on projected budgets.
c) Understand the effect of any alterations you request on the targeted schedule.
d) Zone in on the terms of agreement such as penalties for delays, etc.

When an architect or contractor quotes a rate per square foot, remember that it will only be an approximation. Try to find a way to cap the maximum it could go to. To mitigate the possibility of things getting out of hand later, it is best to review the proposed Bill of Quantities (BOQ) with them in reasonable detail right from the start and on an ongoing basis as well.

While the creative aspects of a concept may develop along the way and the exact detailing of these BOQs may not be possible at the very beginning, this exercise will serve as the 'budgeted rates per square foot' (for each indoor and outdoor space) to benchmark against. This must ideally be done before handing over a signing amount to them, so that the overall expenses stay in line. I have come across situations when an architect's personal design leanings override his objectivity in serving the entrepreneur's time and money agenda. Watching out for such biased personal leanings in an architect is, thus, often more important than his visible architectural accomplishments.

On the other hand, once you have placed your faith in an architect, do give him the freedom to express his creativity.

Good architects with experience, specifically in designing restaurants, can help make tremendous savings to your project through innovative ideas that may save you money on both your capital as well as your operating expenditure. For instance, using an alternate flooring material in a night-only-bar may save you a large amount of capital or, while planning for your HVAC, choosing something which offers economic running costs despite a higher initial capital expenditure, may be prudent.

One entrepreneur whose focus I admire, once said to me about project management, "Saving a few bucks by negotiating down the rate of a particular BOQ is hardly the saving I am looking for since it will most likely result in a corresponding quality compromise by the vendor. I'd rather say that instead of four hinges on that door which jointly cost ₹100, you use three hinges of a higher gauge which jointly cost ₹90 and still do the job well."

Overdoing the cost-saving bit can sometimes work to your disadvantage. In one particular project I worked on with an experienced restaurateur, I found an opportunity to save a good bit of money. However, when I shared the idea with the entrepreneur, I was surprised that he passed up the cost benefit. His view was that once you have already done the due diligence of cost versus quality, don't spend too much time rethinking—just go with it. I went on to discover on many occasions thereafter that he was right. More mistakes happen when you overthink things. Money saving at the cost of poor workmanship or operational efficiency is never worth it.

An architect usually appoints a dedicated project manager to your site to ensure everything is being executed as planned. However, it is necessary that either you or a designated project coordinator from your side, is specifically given the responsibility for liaising on both planning and execution of project work being carried out onsite. Every agency involved may have their limitations, and identifying the cause of delays without directly being involved is difficult.

Some restaurateurs may simply not be in a position to afford an architect at all, and may prefer to design the space themselves. They would need to work extra hard so as to try and work out the aesthetics and functionality of the space themselves.

Creating a collection of reference pictures or sketches for your contractor to execute your vision might assure a good start. I have found that involving your core operational team, including your managers and chefs, is often the best way to ensure the incorporation of functionality into your space. After all, they are the ones who are going to be on the floor actually executing the operation. Ideally, they should be involved in planning functionality right from the early stages.

Whether you have an architect or not, monitoring the work schedule every week is crucial. Once you have received the time-schedule from your contractor, you can track it against actual progress on site. It is best to be present on site yourself to be really cued in to what is actually going on. If it's just not possible, then a representative on your behalf reporting details of what has been completed and what hasn't, is a good idea. Worst case scenario, if neither of these are possible, then remote monitoring via photos sent by your contractor every weekend with a report, may become the only way to measure site progress.

One contractor I worked with had a good system of raising red flags whenever he found his delivery of goods wasn't coming in as planned, or if a larger amount of materials was required than originally estimated on paper. In such situations, the architect and he worked well together and managed to save some good money wherever possible without compromising on the overall look and feel of the space.

I recall one such incident during the project development of a restaurant I helped set up. The architect had envisioned a beautifully-stained Greek style floor matching the theme. However, when it was executed by the contractor, the outcome was far removed from the architect's vision. I learnt later that the complexity was on account of just the right mix of colour coupled with the composition of the cement. Moreover, when it dried up, it looked quite different from when it was wet. We had to do the floor three times over before we got it right. This proved that despite good intentions and competence in execution, more time and money may be spent on some aspects of a project than planned. We simply must accept this and park some budget aside for additional time and money in such eventualities.

Cash flow

An important aspect of project management is cash flow. Simply put, if we don't pay each agency their money as per the agreed schedule, it can lead to expensive delays.

Projecting and planning your monetary requirements for the project well in advance, will save you a lot of headache in terms of how much you need as payouts each month.

Remember that your expense meter begins to tick the moment you decide to go live with your vision. By this time, you'd most likely be paying service providers who are already on board. You would have started paying rent at least partially (some landlords may allow you a rent-free period of say 30 days during the fit-out of your start-up). So, accelerating the overall speed of your project, compressing your start-up time, and opening your restaurant as soon as you are reasonably ready, must be your priority.

Good restaurant design and project monitoring are clearly some of the most crucial factors in translating your restaurant dream into reality. Speedy decision-making and close governance will go a long way towards your overall break-even and profitability.

There will be many times during your project when you will be faced with tough choices. On occasion, it may

Sample Capital Cash Flow Requirement							
Capital Cost	Total Expense	Paid-up	January	February	March	April	May
Landlord Deposit	50,00,000	20,00,000	30,00,000				
Project – Civil	1,00,00,000		30,00,000	40,00,000	20,00,000	10,00,000	
FF&E	60,00,000		30,00,000		30,00,000		
OS&E	40,00,000			10,00,000	30,00,000		
License (one-time)	20,00,000			20,00,000			
Pre-op Expenses	60,00,000		15,00,000	15,00,000	15,00,000	15,00,000	
Consultants	20,00,000	5,00,000	10,00,000	5,00,000			
Fixed-op Expenses	25,00,000		5,00,000	5,00,000	5,00,000	5,00,000	5,00,000
Total	3,75,00,000	25,00,000	1,20,00,000	95,00,000	1,00,00,000	30,00,000	5,00,000

be necessary to choose speed over accuracy in decision-making, and on others, it will be prudent to prioritize accuracy over speed instead (even if it means overshooting your schedule and exceeding your budget).

Reflecting on the future impact of your present decisions, both in the long and short term will help you know when to choose speed and when to choose accuracy. Once you have made a decision, you will have little choice but to embrace its consequences.

Funding and Return on Investment

Having the right amount of funding is very important. A large number of restaurant start-ups fail because they run out of money required to pay for their fixed costs such as rent, electricity, and labour, especially if their early sales don't cover those expenses. So, do remember to allocate sufficient working capital.

Equally important is to be careful of where you secure your funding from. Bringing in the kind of investor who will fund you heavily, but twist your arm after one or two financial quarters is dangerous and frustrating, as their impatience and control over your business may dilute your vision and also take away your creative control.

Self-funding (or bootstrapping), as it's known, is typically the route most first-time restaurateurs take. However, with full control in their hands, comes the entire risk. Partnership is the next best way where you share the risk and the reward.

Angel investors are another route altogether. These high net-worth individuals may choose to invest at an early stage of your business, though even they need to see some level of achievement in your restaurant before they put in any of their money. You could ask around for such people via your chartered accountant or reach out to angel investor networks who bring together business owners and investors on their platforms and help you pitch your idea, provided they are convinced first. Business incubators and accelerator programs are also an option since they help you with advice as well as networking.

Venture capitalists and private equity firms come in only at advanced stages of a business's existence. Bank loans may be possible if you own the property where you intend to start your restaurant.

The restaurant business is not an industry in which all angels and all incubators work. Most are inclined towards investing in technology or other such sectors, so finding them isn't easy, but it's possible if you have a compelling proof of concept.

Viewing your restaurant as an investment

Creating, managing, and financing a restaurant requires the investment of both time and money on the part of the entrepreneur.

- The creator of a start-up requires an innovative bent of mind to develop various aspects of the business, including the menu, service style, ambience, value proposition, business model, etc.

- Managing the restaurant requires a different sort of skill, one more oriented towards the day-to-day activities of the restaurant, its people, and efficiency in its operational systems.
- Financing the business requires an understanding of the monetary deployment of resources, their effective focus, and potential return backed by an appetite for proportionate risk.

It's not often that the first two abilities exist in one entrepreneur and even more rare for one to possess all the three abilities. It is important to recognize the presence or absence of these skills within oneself and either collaborate with other entrepreneurs accordingly, or develop the missing abilities within oneself.

If multiple entrepreneurs or partners are involved, one needs to work out a fair allocation of shareholding that reflects their respective contributions to the business. There is no set norm for such an allocation, as it entirely depends on the needs of the individual and the value (real or perceived) they bring to the business.

For instance, in exchange for the time invested by an entrepreneur or a partner, they may be compensated by way of sweat equity. This equity may be allocated in addition to a basic salary or just by itself. The sweat equity earning partner may invest some money into the firm or may not. It all depends on the agreement between the partners. I have seen sweat equity compensation vary hugely; on occasion, even go up to as much as 50% of the shareholding without any financial investment on the part of this partner.

Regardless of whether it's one partner or more, everyone wants to know what kind of return they may expect on their investment. Unfortunately, here lies one of the biggest myths of the restaurant business.

"Over a hundred percent profit in the restaurant/food business," they sagely declare.

"Who are they?" you may ask.

Two groups of people, mainly:

- Businessmen from other industries who have never read a profit and loss statement of even a single working restaurant, and
- Restaurant industry staff, typically from the lower rung up to the restaurant manager, who may have limited exposure to the profit and loss statements, but clearly no experience in understanding either the business holistically or the dynamics between the numbers.

So, I ask them "Over a hundred percent profit? What do mean by that? My understanding is that profit is a percentage of sales. So, if you have sales of a hundred, you mean half is the profit?"

"Yes, yes," they say enthusiastically. Then I conclude, "So you mean a profit of fifty percent of sales." By now they sheepishly throw in their best defence–"There's no business like the food business. Food is always in demand, even during a recession." I smile knowing that although their logic 'food is always in demand' is true, their conclusion that all restaurants will make it through an economic ebb, or even in a normal market scenario, is completely misplaced. The failure of even some of the most accomplished restaurateurs across the globe during the pandemic or even otherwise stands testimony to that.

For example, Gordon Ramsay's Asian Restaurant, Maze in London, was forced to close doors in 2019 after 14 years of operation since it was no longer financially viable to run. Chef Jamie Oliver—despite his celebrity status and net-worth of hundreds of millions of dollars—could not save his restaurant empire in the UK from collapsing.

Ghantewala, a centuries-old legendary confectionery eatery in Delhi, suffered legal and licensing issues, due to which they had to shut down their operations. The iconic Blue Fox restaurant in Kolkata, which enjoyed tremendous patronage in the 1970s, permanently locked its shutters in 2005 due to labour trouble.

During the pandemic, hundreds of outlets of Subway and Burger King in the United States were forced to close. In India, Anjan Chatterjee—owner of restaurant brands such as Mainland China, Oh! Calcutta, and several such brands across the country—was one of the many well-respected restaurateurs who had to shut down all his loss-making units during the pandemic to remain debt-free.

So, no restaurant or restaurateur, no matter how successful, remains untouched by the intrinsic principles of the industry and the market during regular times or exceptional ones.

On the one hand, there are people who have such unreal expectations, but on the other hand, there are those who deliberately create such an impression to drum up investment in their businesses. By leading investors to believe that they will have healthier returns than are realistically possible, such restaurateurs merely buy themselves a salary and some additional time. After a few financial quarters, when the investors find that things are not going according to their financial projections, they start asking questions—uncomfortable ones. I have often seen restaurateurs forced to strip costs in the eventuality that sales targets remain unachieved. This inevitably comes at the price of reputation. Imagine a situation where you have hired people on the premise that you are going to deliver a certain level of sales, and you have seriously under-delivered, despite your sincere efforts. Now, you are forced to let these people go. The industry is a small place and word spreads. This is not to say that one must be so paralyzed in risk-taking that one never embraces the true spirit of entrepreneurship. Do so indeed, but within reason.

I would like to highlight that in any financial projections you can always estimate your expenses (both capital and operating) to an accuracy of say 10% to 20% more or less, simply by making a few phone calls to the vendors. There is no way, however, that you can accurately estimate your sales in a start-up.

The best way to address this is to put down three or four possible sales scenarios ranging from the best case to the worst case. It is only in this manner that you can study the outcome of each of these scenarios and accordingly prepare for various eventualities of profit and loss, before actually taking the plunge. Remember that your eventual sales-to-investment ratio is pivotal to your business and can make or break your venture.

In terms of financial projections, some experts point out that Return on Investment (ROI) is not an accurate tool to assess the financial feasibility of a restaurant since it does not take into account the time value of money. Internal Rate of Return (IRR), they say, addresses this better. This is indeed true in some ways, but IRR is not a perfect method either.

Just so we are on the same page, ROI is an annual percentage ratio of money gained or lost in proportion to the money initially invested. However, it doesn't indicate how long the investment is retained. IRR is a better indicator of the efficiency, quality, and yield of the investment when comparing it against other investments.

At this point, let's just stick with the simpler ROI option which more people understand and are comfortable with.

So, what is a good percentage of return on investment in the restaurant business? Well, that's certainly a million-dollar question. The fact that we are exploring this matter deeply indicates we are optimistic enough about the returns. What percentage can one expect with restrained optimism?

Let us suppose that in stocks an investor may hope to make a return of say 8% to 12%, then considering the 'extra risk' he is taking with a restaurant, should a return of more than 12% be considered decent? Firstly, let's take a look at what extra risk we are referring to.

The stocks of a public listed company are considered safer since:

1. They can afford to hire a better quality of top management.
2. The investor can make a smaller investment in

stocks, therefore, exposing himself to lesser risk than in a restaurant, and

3. Unless the investor is a day trader, a stock investment will not require daily time involvement.

Based on this, it would be fair to say that for the extra risk taken in investing in a private business, the reward should be higher than 12%–perhaps 15% to 19% might be a decent range. A return of 20% and above would be rather good. Let's try and investigate this a little further.

While individual investors putting in money more casually find this acceptable, institutional investors may expect a return ranging from say 25% to 50% or even more. Angel investors investing in the early stages of a business may look for ten times the original investment in seven years, though it's not necessary that they will stay invested for that long.

I've seen renowned restaurant brands make as low as 7% to 8% returns and still carry on since they would like to be present in a certain market, and sometimes relatively lesser known brands earn returns as high as 30% quite consistently. I have also heard of some restaurants making higher than 30% though haven't seen any myself. Most industry people I have spoken with from around the globe, seem to feel that a return on investment of somewhere around 20% per annum is good in the restaurant business. Clearly, a restaurateur and an investor, particularly one not from the industry, may have different expectations of their return on investment.

In terms of payback period, while many bravely say that the profit of 18 months or less should cover the capital expenditure, I have found practically that somewhere between 18 and 36 months is a good enough payback period. If you have a way of assuring a certain level of sales, let's say a firm commitment from a certain number of office goers nearby, then you may have a basis of gauging your payback period. In normal circumstances, however, remember that if your expected sales targets aren't achieved for any reason, your payback will just drag on painfully. If you manage to achieve payback in less than a year and a half, that's excellent.

Furthermore, you should know that even the same brand in different locations may have differing ROIs and payback periods. ROI is not a static percentage which remains constant year after year. In the start-up year it may be say 8%, then it may go up to 15%, then 24% where it plateaus for let's say three years and then it may even drop to 18%.

High net-worth individuals, company professionals, sportspersons, and even celebrities looking to invest in options other than conventional investment vehicles, often look at start-up businesses to punt on. They may either be passionate about the restaurant business or simply be looking for a 'high risk–high reward' alternative. A restaurateur must be selective about the nature of the investor he chooses to work with. Remember, that by virtue of his shareholding right, such an investor may be in a position to completely alter the nature of decisions in your business, which in turn will affect its success or failure.

The decision to make an investment in any kind of

business is usually based on the investor's judgement as to whether or not the company's leadership and value proposition will be strong enough to make inroads into the market place in a manner that is likely to deliver success to all its stakeholders.

To be more specific, let's take a look at a typical list of criteria that angel investors or venture capitalists tend to look for before investing in a restaurant:

Team quality:

Individual team members' leadership experience, domain expertise, track record, passion, commitment, open mindedness, and team likeability.

Market potential:

The quality of the solution that the value proposition offers to a market problem leads to either a lot of consumers wanting a little of it, or attracts a few consumers wanting a lot of it. For a start-up, validation through a pilot test in the marketplace with evidence of a favourable response makes investors more confident. In a growth scenario, validation through a proof of concept is considered a more reliable basis for an investment decision rather than just a gut call.

Financials:

Scale of investment, duration of investment, promoter's proportion of financial investment otherwise known as 'skin in the game', investment schedule.

Business model:

Revenue model with income plan, sales and marketing

plan for achievement of targets, growth potential and scalability, risk and mitigation, exit plan.

Brand differentiation:

The creative signature-characteristics your brand delivers provide an added benefit to its patrons over your existing and potential competitors. For e.g., patented recipes, processes, etc.

Before going live with your restaurant, I find it makes good business sense to invest time in reflecting on, validating, and detailing each point on this list.

Having said that, I would like to point out that getting too bogged down by any of these criteria can be self-defeating, and, in fact, even lead to disaster. Let's take the 'scalability' criteria, for example. A brand promoter I once worked with owned a deli beautifully modelled around the McDonald's food production philosophy. Pancake batter was poured into perfect moulds at prescribed temperatures for prescribed durations of time on each side of the pancake to prepare it. Every aspect of the deli's food, service, and ambience was planned perfectly... except for one.

We were losing money month after month and the key reason was our high prices. It was the high cost of our raw materials that forced us to raise prices to a level that our target audience found unacceptable. The high price resulted in two things: It restricted the target audience from visiting the place in large numbers, and those who patronized it, inevitably got irked and found 'something not quite right' about the food. The simple fact was that they could get a tastier and cheaper version within a stone's throw. Worried about the way things were going, I expressed my concern to the promoter.

I was shocked to learn that since he wanted the business to necessarily be scalable, he believed that it was necessary to buy raw materials of a 'higher standard', even if the procurement from another city meant higher costs, an initial uncertain lead time, and a temporary loss.

I pointed out to him that if we were losing money by serving an average quality product at a high price in one outlet, many outlets could at best get us a small discount on products of the same average quality. Scaling up our outlets, therefore, was not going to get any significant volume discount for us to suddenly start becoming profitable.

I also expressed my dissent at having to pay transportation charges from one city to another and expecting our customers to pay more for that, when they had better quality alternatives available. Strangely, he just didn't get it and continued losing money till he was forced to shut down his brand. So, as an investor he insisted so much on the scalability parameter, that he couldn't get even one outlet working right.

Ironically, this is not just an issue with a few people, but with most of us when we wear our investor hats. To avoid getting caught in such a trap, it is best to work with a mentor who is likely to show you where your vision might be getting constricted.

While disciplined logic is clearly the soundest basis on which one should make investment decisions, I must mention that, at times, I have also witnessed such decisions succeeding despite them being based purely on instinct or even emotion. Such instances, however, have been rare and inevitably backed up with the presence of strong resources and tremendous resilience within the organization.

If you are seeking to invest your time and money to create a brand only to hand over the reins to someone else, or even if you have the ability to run a brand you created, or are looking after an existing one, you may need to consider a restaurant management arrangement.

Sample of a Proposed Restaurant Management Agreement

Brand Owner Benefits	Brand Operator Benefits
- Reduced time investment - No dealing with day-to-day operations - Retain brand ownership - Possible increased profit	- No financial investment - Uses expertise and/or time to grow - Earns fees

Brand Owner Responsibilities	Brand Operator Responsibilities
- To finance capital expenditure - To finance working capital (for opening) - To handle legal matters - To handle property matters - To handle insurance matters - To handle banking matters	- To plan and execute sales and marketing initiatives - To manage expenses and profit - To manage and motivate manpower - To manage and maintain accounts - To manage hygiene and sanitation - To maintain machines and other business assets - To manage vendors and inventory - To manage customers and brand sanctity - To maintain the sanctity of intellectual property (non-compete clause sign-off by the operator)

Sample operator fee:

1. Management fee:

a)   A fixed amount – for control and reporting of MIS (cash, inventory, etc.) to the brand owner, plus

b)   A variable amount – 3% to 7% of sales (net of taxes).

2. Incentive:

Around 15% to 25% of profit in case of a surplus in profit over and above the budgeted profit. For e.g., if the budgeted profit is 25% and the profit achieved is 35%, then this fee will be calculated on the 10% differential profit.

3. Out-of-pocket expenses:

Expenses such as major repairs, irregular expenses, or any other similar expenses as mutually agreed upon between the owner and the operator.

Planning Your Restaurant

Here is an example of a business plan, including its concept and financials, followed by a decision on whether or not to act upon the idea.

Name of business

Plant-Based Food Café

Owner/s

You

Statement of purpose

We are a vegan café, focussed on fulfilling the newfound need of urban India with healthy and fresh plant-based food. The mock egg, dairy, and chicken dishes served will be purely plant-based.

Explanation of purpose

Consumers today value brands that offer freshness, quality, traceability, standardization, local ingredients, societal benefits, sustainable materials, etc. A study of the post-pandemic boom of plant-based foods in urban India reveals the mushrooming number of such cafes in the city. Being one of the early brands serving this demand is in line with the current trend which seems likely to have a future.

Achieving the experience

Food

- A consulting chef will be hired to develop the menu and work out the recipes, their costing and selling price, the equipment, and staff required. Should the project look feasible, the chef will then train line cooks on dishing out that menu.
- Some ingredients that are not yet available in the city would need to be sourced and a back-up plan for vendors put in place.
- Self-service (except for clearance of dirty dishes, service of beverages, and the bill).

Service

A hybrid model which incorporates the speed and efficiency of a McDonald's, with the guest-feel and experience of a Starbucks.

Ambience

White walls embellished with wall paintings and pictures of green earth, farms, plants, and nature. Wooden panelling with bright and cheery lighting.

Target audience

Well-travelled global citizens who comprise of top-tier professionals, including corporate executives, business owners, film stars, etc.

- First timers and early adopters who would like to experience what plant-based food tastes like.
- Non-vegetarians taking a break from non-veg, egg, or dairy for health or religious reasons.
- Vegans, vegetarians, and environmentalists who want to consume a steady plant-based or vegan diet.

Space break-up

Total area = 1000 sq. ft.

Front of the House (dining, cash counter, display if any, guest toilet) = 700 sq. ft.

Back of the House (kitchen, stores, staff area, office) = 300 sq. ft.

Number of covers/seats = 35

Business location

Prime locations like Bandra West or Nepean Sea Road where our audience resides. Apart from the café, if additional space is required, it may be considered in cheaper premises in the vicinity.

Hours of operation

Timings would be 7 a.m. to 11 p.m. covering breakfast, lunch, and dinner service.

Annual holidays would need to be defined in advance based on practicality. For example: the day of Ganpati immersion where few people venture out, or a yearly staff picnic on a relatively slow weekday.

Menu

(All egg, dairy, and chicken dishes are plant-based substitutes.)

Breakfast

- Scrambled Eggs with spinach, mushroom, and breakfast roll.
- Masala Omelette with tomato, broccoli, and breakfast roll.
- Oatmeal raisin with almond milk and seasonal fruit.
- Amaranth Porridge with rice milk, nuts, seeds, and berries.

Snacks

- Loaded Nacho Platter with cheese and tomato sauce.
- Corn Cheese Poppers with salad.
- Hummus Platter with pesto, beet, and crackers.
- Bruchetta (six pieces) with microgreens.

Mains – International

- Bowls of Thai Curry with Rice–Veggie/Chicken.
- Pasta-Veggie/Chicken (with option of white sauce or red sauce).

Mains – Indian

- Bowls (with rice/mini naan)–Butter Paneer Masala/ Butter Chicken.
- Masala/Dal Bukhara.
- Malabar Paratha Rolls (with salad and pickle) – Paneer/Chole/Kheema.

Salad Bowls

- Apple Feta Salad with cucumber, olives, and almond slivers.
- Pad Thai flat noodles with edamame, purple cabbage, and peanut dressing.

Drinks

- Iced Tea/Fresh lime Water.
- Shakes–Strawberry/Chocolate/Cold Coffee.

Dessert

- Warm Bread Pudding.
- Rich Chocolate Mousse.

Your business plan is most sound when it is based on market research that you conduct yourself or with an agency, in addition to generically published market research that you may have considered (since it may be outdated).

Projected Financials

Capital Expenditure

Account Head	Details	Amount
Air-conditioning	40 tons @ ₹30,000	1,200,000
Exhaust	Kitchen and restaurant	200,000
Water	Purifier and cooler	50,000
Kitchen equipment		1,800,000
Civil work	Incl. furniture, stores, and staff toilet	2,800,000
Service equipment		400,000
Uniforms and linen		200,000
Staff lockers		25,000
Computers		400,000
Telephones		100,000
Licensing	One-time cost	500,000
Gas	Bank and ducting	100,000
Architects fee	@ 10% of related project cost	500,000
Deposit	For premises	1,000,000
Consultants fee	Lump sum	300,000
Contingencies	Approximately @ 5% of project cost	500,000
Total		10,075,000

Working Capital per month

Running Costs	(when operational) Amount	(during development) Amount	% of operational
Rent	150,000	150,000	100%
Salaries	300,000	150,000	50%
Electricity	100,000	30,000	30%

Water	5,000	1,500	30%
Licenses and permissions	15,000	15,000	100%
Marketing and advertising	20,000	20,000	100%
Maintenance and décor	25,000	-	
Telephone and fax	20,000	20,000	100%
Transport	15,000	15,000	100%
Staff welfare	15,000	7,500	50%
Food/Alcohol @ 35% of sales	672,000	-	
Contingency @ 5% of sales	96,000	48,000	50%
Total costs per month	1,433,000	457,000	

Sales

Meal breakup –Time-wise	Daily Covers		
Lunch	30		
Dinner	120		
Total	150		
Meal breakup – Item-wise	Daily Covers	Avg. bill per person	Daily Sales
Food only	110	400	44,000
Food & Beer	40	500	20,000
Total	150	Total	64,000
Monthly Sales	1,920,000		

Less Costs per month	1,433,000		
Monthly Profit	487,000		

Budget

Capital Expenditure	10,075,000
Working Capital up to opening (9 months)	4,113,000
Total Startup Cost	14,188,000
Annual Profit	5,844,000
Breakeven occurs in approximately	29 months

The Problem with Cloud Kitchens

A cloud kitchen, known as a 'restaurant without a dining area', is basically a kitchen focussed on producing food for fast pick-up and delivery. It is inevitably in a low-cost locality, invisible to its guests physically, but highly visible online and connected digitally—thus the word 'cloud'.

A single cloud kitchen may serve as the production facility for many different online brands offering diverse dishes, ranging from pizza, biryani to Chinese food, under the same roof. While the equipment, ingredients, and production staff may or may not be different in each brand, it shares common resources that bring in economies of scale. For instance, common staff and space for receiving raw materials can also be used for preparing food, dispatching the take-out orders, washing area, etc.

The capital expenditure and monthly costs of running a cloud kitchen are significantly lower than that of a regular restaurant. This is because of the lower costs of real estate as compared to that in a mall or the high street, less space and staff requirement since there is no dining area, and lower cost of equipment and furniture as a cloud kitchen is not visible to its patrons.

With a focus primarily on production and delivery, a cloud kitchen is built to have the capability of cooking in large volumes and delivering food quickly and widely, and thus, generating good sales volumes at significantly lower costs.

These reasons make the cloud kitchen model an attractive one… even aspirational, and draws the interest of existing operators and new ones—large and small—with a dream of making it big. Stories of success have been fuelled by the food and beverage operators who have received millions in funding, leading to the conclusion that if investors are betting so high on it, it must certainly be worth investing in.

Consultants and other professionals speak and write volumes about how lucrative this business is and how they can help you set up. Herein lies the problem….

What you should know is: while the capital and running costs of a cloud kitchen are indeed lower than that of a dine-in restaurant, your fixed costs of rent, electricity, and labour, however low, still need to be covered through adequate sales.

You will be told about how easily aggregators can provide you plug and play marketing and sales platforms, delivery services, and billing facilities. Unfortunately, less is being said about the price of these advertising and discounting packages (in addition to their commissions of over 25%)

and other services. And especially for a new unknown brand, incurring these heavy expenses of aggregators become essential for your menu to show up high within your category on their platform.

Competing with food brands of long-standing repute and with well-funded kitchens (at times owned by the aggregators themselves), makes it very hard for even highly committed professionals and entrepreneurs with some financial backing to survive, let alone make a worthwhile profit. If you don't think this through, you might as well be on your way to lose your hard-earned savings.

If you're exploring an opportunity in the cloud kitchen space, check three things:

1. Current players in the market who have a strong existing brand (well-known restaurant chains, five-star hotels, reputed tiny eateries, etc.), or, deep pockets (well-funded aggregators, for example) with the ability to burn cash and offer huge discounts for even a decade, or another such strength. Are you **strong enough** to compete with them?

2. One of the greatest reasons for failure in this sector is timing. Many other entrepreneurs may have already rolled out similar concepts to what you have in mind. Are you **early enough** to exploit the opportunity or is it too late?

3. If you believe you have something unique (however small) that can't easily be replicated by others, by all means, launch your enterprise. I'm all for a new 'venture'. Are you **distinctive enough** to start with and what will you do if someone copies you?

Broadly speaking, most food endeavours across the world taste failure from time to time. While consumers certainly benefit from the aggressive competition for their hearts and wallets, I worry that in today's environment, even more food start-ups (than the pre-pandemic era) will fail and erode wealth rather than create it.

So, ask not whether you can start a cloud kitchen, since you most certainly can. Ask instead, whether you can make a profit in this business and, if so, how and how sustainably.

To Start or Not To…

> In any investment decision, planning and preparation is of the essence. As Thomas Edison once pointed out—*"Good fortune is what happens when opportunity meets with planning."*

A wise man once told me that for a concept to succeed, it should be either something very common or then very uncommon.

Once you have your business plan in place, i.e., your concept and financial projections, it's time for you to take a decision on whether or not to start the business. That is, either you actually go live with it, or, you decide to abort the plan. Both decisions take a lot of courage.

If you have discovered along the way, through your research and understanding of the industry, that you want to be a restaurateur with the concept you have finalized, then it's time for you to head to Section 2.

Alternately, if you find that though you have decided to be a restaurateur, the concept you have shortlisted doesn't work, then you'll need to start over and come up with a new concept. Please don't be harsh on yourself in such a situation. It's quite normal to work on multiple concepts before your instinct tells you which one is right for you and for the market.

On the other hand, if you find that the restaurant business doesn't suit you well considering the kind of commitment it requires in terms of time, money, etc., it is best that you face the reality and pursue something else instead.

I have helped many such entrepreneurs let go of their restaurant dream when they realize it is not meant for them. Imagine if you did not go through this exercise to evaluate yourself and instead discovered it after you invested a lot of time, money, and passion into it, how much worse it would be. My endeavour with this book is to save you that financial and emotional pain.

To start or not to start is a matter of logic, instinct, or both. Beyond a point one cannot overthink it. One simply has to either abort the idea or take the plunge.

On the premise that you are going to continue your pursuit of the restaurant business and you would like to delve deeper, let's move on to 'Going Live'.

Section II

Going Live

To ensure that your restaurant runs smoothly, it is essential to have a system where each activity is effectively handled by the right person, with the least time, effort, and money spent. Efficiency is the key here.

Time Costs Money

It is critical to understand the role of time and money management in the efficient execution of a project setup. Every day that a project runs behind time, it costs you dearly in terms of money.

Delays on account of dependency on authorities, suppliers, landlords, or employees are frustrating but natural. You will find it best to budget for more time than your estimated schedule and then work within that as far as possible. Delays of payments due from your end will cost you time. Unfortunately, settling your suppliers' dues on time does not necessarily ensure timely delivery from their end.

Some techniques to improve efficiency include:

- Make 'to-do lists' for your short- and long-term goals.
- Develop detailed checklists for each department by listing individual tasks to be performed. Prioritize while ticking off completed responsibilities and adding new ones. Delegate wherever possible.
- Make a 'Time and Cash Flow schedule' of tasks to be completed before you start.

Remember that you are your number one employee and keep yourself motivated; using positive reinforcement (e.g., reminding yourself of successfully completed tasks) may be rewarding.

Each day you will have to perform multiple tasks simultaneously. A chart capturing them will help you plan and monitor the project from beginning to end.

Time management

Here are some ways you could categorize your tasks to effectively manage them:

Progress vs. Maintenance tasks

Maintenance tasks are those required to sustain your existing position, while progress tasks are those that are likely to improve on it.

Important vs. Urgent tasks

Prioritize your tasks based on how important and urgent they are. Some may be important but not urgent, and vice

Task Schedule

Weeks

Tasks	1	2	3	4	5	6	7	8	9	10	11	12	13	14	15	16	17	18	19	20
Ducting	█	█																		
Cabling			█	█																
Final Plastering					█															
Painting																				
Recruitment	█	█	█	█	█	█	█	█	█	█	█									
Staff Training									█	█	█	█	█	█	█	█	█	█		
Linen													█	█	█					
Cutlery / Crockery																				
Licensing	█	█	█	█	█	█	█	█	█	█	█	█	█	█	█	█	█	█	█	█
Food trials									█	█	█	█	█	█	█	█	█	█		
Credit card machine															█	█				
Supplier contracts																				

versa. The ones that are both, important and urgent, need to be at the top of the list.

Planning the Menu

Once we decide on the menu and estimate the amount of each dish to be cooked, we can figure out what equipment we will require—their capacities, whether they need to be customized or bought off the shelf, should they be imported from abroad or from domestic sources, etc.

Irrespective of the food and beverage concept, a menu is a great way of communicating the establishment's offer to a patron. It must thus be created, developed, and managed thoughtfully. Begin with the customer in mind. A combination of familiar items, new innovations, and signature dishes, make guests feel comfortable and engaged with a brand.

Once the target market for the business has been identified, a menu development team must be formed. Besides a chef, this team should include a business head, marketing manager, and an accounts manager. They could jointly look into existing consumer preferences and possible future trends to arrive at broad cuisines, 'must-have' dishes, their costs, selling prices, presentation, etc.

After trying out dishes internally, food trials may be conducted for a cross section of people from the target market with a view to incorporating their feedback. This gives us leads on which dishes, tastes, colours, textures, portion sizes, aromas, etc., are likely to work in our favour. We can then tweak the menu accordingly.

The menu mix of an organization helps it stand out from others on the market. Chefs must make that additional effort to deploy every possible resource to stimulate the senses of the patrons.

Menu finalization allows us to plan the equipment, workforce, and other resources required to produce the food. It also paves the way for calculating food cost.

While the desired overall food cost of a particular restaurant could be, let's say 23% to 33%, your food cost for each dish can be whatever you want it to be. How? You can control the food cost percentage of a dish by choosing an appropriate selling price. So, if you wish to offer greater value to your patron by selling a dish costing ₹25, for ₹75 instead of ₹100, your food cost percentage changes from 25% to 33%. There will always be some dishes that you sell at a low margin and others you sell for a high profit. Eventually, it is the weighted average percentage that matters to the establishment.

It's also important to take note of the price-to-portion size ratio of each dish from a market acceptance viewpoint before arriving at a final decision. We could look at restaurants that have similar cuisine and positioning as ours for reference. This helps to ensure that our offer is in sync with the market.

While the menu is being finalized, options to present it online or as a physical card may be discussed with the creative team. Menu card materials and design elements could be selected based on the overall concept and target market. The number of physical copies required will depend on the scale of operation, level of formality in service, method of presentation, and the frequency of making new menus.

In a start-up, guesstimates of what percentage each dish on the menu will contribute to the sales are rarely accurate. In an existing F&B concept, however, historic records allow us to understand which dishes are most or least popular, which contribute the most or least towards the sales and which contribute the most or least towards the profits. In a running operation, the accounts department plays a crucial role in highlighting which dish does what for the establishment in terms of profitability, and also for the guest in terms of popularity.

On the matter of menu variety, it is important to keep a balance between what your guests might actually want, and what is feasible to make with the resources you have.

The expectations of your patrons for a particular dish are based on their previous experience of that dish served in other establishments, or the way your item is described in the menu. If the delivery doesn't meet their expectations, then it most certainly leads to disappointment.

Imagination plays a great role in the enjoyment of food. When developing a menu, the primary aim is to create a sensory anticipation in the mind of your guest.

Whether to offer an à la carte or table d'hôte menu would depend on the hours of operation, staff availability, guest requirements, and your vision for the place. So, it would be best to first present a tentative list of options to test groups for sampling. These groups must represent the target market you intend to serve. Based on their responses you may retain, eliminate, or alter dishes.

Guests tire quickly of the same menu, and every once in a while, need to see innovative changes. One should work in conjunction with the chef to arrive at an interesting array of dishes based on:

- Sensory appeal
- Nutritional value
- Seasonal availability
- Cost of production
- The Chef's specialities

Good food is the soul of your restaurant and a great chef its backbone. Finding someone who is creative yet practical may be your greatest challenge. It is important to remember that the more exclusive the cuisine, the less replaceable the chef. To ensure chef retention you could consider a profit-sharing scheme. It is also important to standardize recipes to assure consistency in the taste and quality of food.

A 'Standardized Recipe Card' helps each member of your kitchen team deliver that dish in the exact same way, each time. This helps you stay consistent with your brand promise rather than have some maverick cook thinking he will cook it his way and ending up disappointing your patrons.

Standardized Recipe Card

Name of the dish:	____________________
No. of portions:	_______
Cooking time:	_______
Total production time:	_______
Temperature:	_______
Service dish:	____________________
Accompaniment:	____________________

Ingredients	Quantity	Method

Cost of Food = ____________________

Labour = ____________________

Overheads = ____________________

Total cost of production = ____________________

Cost per portion = Cost of production / No. of portions =

____

Listening to your patrons and adapting accordingly is one of the most basic yet accurate ways of tweaking your menu to meet their expectations. A team that keeps their ears to the ground (on the menu front) will go a long way in retaining the interest of their patrons and maximizing earnings for their brand.

Managing Purchase and Stores

You need to follow the path of each item you require in terms of its quality, quantity, and cost, as is said in the food industry, 'from farm to plate'.

So:

1. Make a checklist of what you need.
2. Decide on your vendors (keep a back-up, in case one ditches you).
3. Monitor your storage.
4. Issue items from the stores to the kitchen.
5. Cook and serve dishes on your menu.
6. Check the yield and keep an eye on wastage.
7. Review the item-wise profitability.

The storage area usually has sections at different temperatures: ambient for groceries; refrigerated for produce, dairy, etc.; freezer for meats, etc., apart from separate storage for liquor—both at room temperature and refrigerated—as allocated by the excise department.

Suitable ventilation and drainage would also have to be kept in mind in the stores. It goes without saying that an honest and experienced Purchase and Stores Executive could help you with his market understanding, goodwill for credit, and save you a good bit in profit.

It is best to follow the 'First In First Out' method of storekeeping. Items entering your store room first would be the most perishable ones and hence should be utilized first.

Furthermore, to keep track of purchases, a chef or an employee of any department must fill in a requisition for it.

Purchase Requisition			
Sr. No.: _____　　Date: _______　　Department: __________			
No.	Item	Quantity	Description
Required by date: __________　　　Department head signature: __________			

To run a kitchen well you need to:

- Schedule a daily and monthly cleaning and maintenance program.
- Manage energy effectively, e.g., tracking freezer temperature.
- Keep hygiene accessories, including soap, sanitizers, and paper towels, handy.
- Define procedures to be implemented, such as:

  1. Separate chopping boards/storage for meat, fish, and vegetables to prevent cross-contamination.
  2. No fat in sink drains to avoid clogging.
  3. Use of protective gear such as chef caps, bandages, and gloves.

You need to create your own system to analyze every operational function and its path. How you will add or subtract items from the menu, how raw materials will be stored, how wastage will be managed, how accounting will be done, etc., should be thought out well in advance.

Based on their prior experience, each department head could outline policies and procedures in the form of an operations manual. This would serve as a guide for the staff and could be updated based on further inputs. However, one must realize that certain situations may require an employee to make decisions on the spot other than those prescribed.

To avoid communication problems, it is best to inform suppliers of the specifics of our requirement. For example, the kind and size of tomato we want (how many in a kilo), and so on.

The chef of a restaurant company I once worked with once called me in desperation–"Our cheese vendor refuses to deliver due to non-payment of previous dues, I have no back-up and cheese being primary to our menu, I can't work without it." Knowing the company to be quite cash-rich, I was surprised that non-payment could be the reason. I first asked the chef to verify whether we had received and consumed the materials that the vendor claimed he had sent us. After a few moments, he confirmed with his team that the materials had indeed been received and consumed. I then called the accounts department to understand their perspective. Surprisingly, they had no idea about these materials received and still due to be paid for. It was evident that there was no procedure for recording goods received at the restaurant and communicating the details to the accounts team. The solution was to ensure a daily update of both the accounts and the purchase departments on these matters.

A 'Goods Received Register' serves just this purpose and helps maintain a record of actual consumption as well as the smooth release of payments to vendors, thus preventing the occurrence of such operational issues.

Goods Received Register									
Date	Sup-plier Name	Bill No.	De-part-ment	Item	Unit	Rate	Bin card	Amount Cash/ Credit	Remarks

When taking an order, the service staff concerned must write down details of patrons' instructions. Food items must be noted on the Kitchen Order Ticket (K.O.T) and drinks on the Bar Order Ticket (B.O.T).

Kitchen Order Ticket		
Sr. No.: _____	Date: _________	Time: _________
Table No.: _____	No. of covers: _____	Order-taker: _________
Item	Quantity	Remarks / Alterations
		Signature: _________

Managing Performance

"What cannot be measured cannot be managed," is a well-known mantra in the business world. Yet, Albert Einstein famously said, "Not everything that counts can be measured. Not everything that can be measured counts."

Creating a restaurant management system that enables you to define, monitor, and achieve your business objectives through the right strategies and tactics is thus crucial to managing the performance of your restaurant.

A useful tool that you can develop and use to manage your restaurant is a dashboard report. Just as a car dashboard gives its driver a real-time perspective of vehicle performance for effective decisions, a restaurant dashboard gives a restaurateur a real-time perspective of his business performance for effective decisions.

It is important to choose only those objectives for measurement that will help you achieve your business vision, while satisfying your customers. For example, if your business vision is to build a restaurant with an authentic music-driven experience, your initiatives must be prioritized, and your resources focused accordingly. This means that the necessary infrastructure must be woven into your business model in a manner that will attract music lovers.

Every organization's vision and goals are unique so the metrics to measure them and the initiatives taken to achieve them must also be unique. One solution certainly cannot fit all. For instance, a McDonald's may find it critical to include metrics that diligently measure and manage its delivery of customer nutrition as opposed to many other restaurants that don't find it necessary, at least as of date.

Working with a restaurant dashboard consistently leads to systematically increasing operational efficiency, thereby enhancing the effective delivery of value to your patrons and ultimately to your shareholders.

The key performance indicators in your dashboard besides the obvious sales, costs, and profit, may include the happiness quotient of your patrons, employees, vendors, and the community around you.

Finding the right hardware and software will allow you to put in place the systems that will help you track these things routinely. However, a system is only as good as its people.

Putting Together Your Team

"You're only as good as the people you hire."

–Ray Kroc

Employees are the ones who actualize your goals—whether in finance, marketing, or operations. Without them your vision would remain only a dream. In the hospitality industry, the interaction between customer and restaurant employee takes on a special meaning and importance, and customer satisfaction depends almost entirely on a smooth performance from the staff. A single inattentive steward could damage the reputation of your restaurant. It is therefore most important to attract the right kind of employees, induct them into your brand values and vision, engage, support and reward them, keep them motivated, and do what it takes to retain them.

The first thing you need to do is to list out the functions that your organization needs to perform. Then determine the number of people (and their backgrounds) that are necessary to achieve this aim.

Your first employees may include a manager and a chef whose expertise could be utilized in the further planning and hiring of your work force.

Creating a job description for each role that outlines details of the role to be played by each employee brings clarity about what actually needs to get done by each person. Once you have thought through what each employee must 'deliver', you could consider the possible sources of hiring personnel. While I typically prefer spreading the word about requirement of staff through referrals or hiring a placement firm, candidates may be attracted through advertisements in newspapers or online. Incentivizing existing employees with a cash bonus if the person they refer is hired also works well.

What the employee expects:

- **Fair treatment:** A no tolerance policy towards abuse of any sort—something that's known to happen in the industry.
- **Equitable pay:** High wages don't necessarily satisfy employees, but low wages certainly dissatisfy them.
- **Reasonable work hours:** While some are still willing to work long hours for overtime or do break-shifts

(For e.g., 11 a.m. to 3 p.m. – break – 7 p.m. to 11 p.m.); bringing in a good amount of straight shifts, (For e.g., 3 p.m. to midnight), helps.

- **Staff welfare:** Basic safety—tested equipment, fire exits, etc., good timely staff meals, preferably before feeding the patrons, employee insurance, etc.,—must be ensured.
- **Growth opportunities:** Succession planning at all levels helps create a talent pool within and is in the organization's own interest.
- **Meaningful work:** A sense of purpose gives each employee a depth to their responsibility and accountability.

Employees, like guests, have an option to go elsewhere. Finding the right employee for the position the first time around would be your most prudent choice. To attract and retain the best in the market, you need to create the right work environment in your establishment.

A résumé is an indication of the candidate's ability and potential. Whether it undersells him or oversells him, only an interview will tell. It gives an insight into how the applicant projects himself and shows the values he holds high. Going through it carefully leads to putting together the questions you will ask him in the interview.

Innovative reward and recognition programmes generally boost morale and sustain interest over longer periods. You may provide perks such as overtime, medical allowance, staff transport, incentives on increased volumes of business, flexible schedules, an annual picnic, a prize for employee of the month, educational assistance, annual bonus, etc.

A consistent effort over time will develop your reputation as a serious restaurateur committed to high standards of food service management. Now, you can have your choice of the best employees in the business.

Bringing In the Money

So, you have planned how much capital you need and figured out your best and worst case sales scenarios for the business. Don't forget working capital. Before you open the doors of your restaurant, you would need pre-opening working capital which will cover your fixed costs when your business is just a project. Once you open your doors and start getting enough sales to cover your fixed costs (rent, electricity, labour), you will need to budget for post-opening working capital.

The next thing to remember if you are self-funded is that besides the capital you would also need to factor in your own living expenses—add that to the equation. Just to be on the safe side, be sure to put aside enough to last you for at least a year.

If you have borrowed money, you must have a plan in place to pay it back with interest. Ensure adequate time from your financier in case things take longer than planned. More importantly, as with any investment, know how much you can afford to lose. Hope for the best, but prepare for the worst.

If things go as planned, or near enough that you're making a profit, then you need to be prepared to run your restaurant day after day. While you need tremendous persistence to reach this point, the stamina required to continually run a restaurant for years thereafter is something else altogether.

So, let's look at what it takes to run a restaurant.

Section III

Running Your Restaurant

Serving quality food at a great value day after day with a smile is the only way diners return and new ones hear about it.

Delivering this requires an almost military-like discipline, but with a heart. This need for daily consistency is why Standard Operating Procedures (SOPs) need to be developed and followed. It is also the reason why your team is a critical part of your success. So, let's look at the management of operations, people, money, branding, and marketing.

An Overall Management Checklist

- Figure out what you hope to achieve through your venture creatively, socially, and financially. Then work out a business plan comprising every crucial step needed to achieve it.
- Keep a constant watch on which goals are being met, which aren't and why, so you can work on them better. Ease in communication between team members helps in quick responses.

- Computerize your systems wherever feasible with a manual back-up whenever possible. Install quality software systems that could help facilitate day-to-day operations of your restaurant. A good management information system serves as a dashboard for decision-making and problem-solving.

- Create a healthy work environment with well-defined job responsibilities, upgradation of skills, and performance-linked rewards to attract and retain staff. Establish a shift hand-over schedule, but also have a back-up plan for when key employees are absent or on leave.

- Be clear on the restaurant image you wish to portray. Have a guest attraction, retention, and reward plan in place.

- Exercise tight control over goods purchased, received, stored, and issued. Monitor recipe standardization, actual yield, wastage, and portion size. Regularly follow cost control and cost reduction practices.

- Devise an effective property management system with adherence to hygiene standards, a firefighting plan, periodic pest control, security plan, equipment warranty/contract register, and a preventive maintenance program.

- Maintain a folder of all legal documents like agreements, insurance, licenses, etc.

Standard Operating Procedures (SOPs)

At most restaurants I worked and knew, SOP manuals were rarely followed. They were looked upon as something that is theoretical and idealistic. Industry leaders and management would lament about how great things would be if policies were actually followed and team members would point out that many policies were highly impractical.

I realized that there was merit on both sides and endeavoured to find a balance.

Clearly, a good-looking and glorious sounding manual will be impractical and unimpressive to investors or franchisees if your own team admits that it's just for show. How then should policies be formed in the first place and how best can they actually be implemented?

Over the years, it became evident to me that unless policies were created differently, their implementation would leave a lot to be desired. Here are five aspects I focussed on in organizations that I worked with, which I found helped improve implementation substantially. I must mention upfront that they were extremely tedious to execute; attempting to transform mindsets always is.

However, if you can see this as a painful yet necessary exercise, pivotal in achieving what has been eluding you for a long time, do give it a try. It will indeed bear fruit and you will gradually experience its value.

Here's how I recommend you see and manage your SOPs well:

1. Define your goal

When defining a goal, it is best that you make it the loftiest one possible. In this case let's say it's, "The implementation of desired procedures in the absence of superiors." We all know how differently teams behave in front of their leaders, and behind their backs. After all, CCTVs can't capture all of it and even if they did, who's sitting to watch them beginning to end?

2. Identify the priorities

Don't try to list every possible policy and procedure that can be written in a SOP manual. This will surely fail. Instead, make a list of only those areas of the business in which you need to make new policies or revise old ones. Those causing the most impact to your organization would be the best place to start with. If you are a start-up, identify and list out only those policies that are most necessary for the initial period. If you are an existing organization, identify and list the greatest pain points in your company that need to be addressed.

In either case, you would need to look at matters of concern from various perspectives:

- From the company's perspective (e.g., In an existing restaurant: A high level of simultaneous and extended leave periods taken by many of the staff members).
- From the guest's perspective (e.g., In an existing restaurant: The service isn't fast enough).
- From the team's perspective (e.g., In a start-up restaurant: How much staff welfare is adequate?).
- From the vendor's perspective (e.g., In a start-up restaurant: How agreed payment schedules can be regularly met).

This would be a holistic way to create a set of priorities to work on with your team.

3. Ensure practicality of policies

Once you have selected your causes, you must dissect their rationale.

A series of meetings with your core team becomes necessary for this. Taking time out from day-to-day operations is tremendously useful. Honest and focussed meetings can end both long- standing as well as severe issues with finality.

Encourage discussions and debates in your team on every aspect of a solution from a viewpoint of practical operations, their financial impact, legal implications, etc. Once all or at least most parties involved are satisfied with what the most appropriate solution is, the first draft of that policy can be formulated in writing. Often policies may be met with great resistance. Think through which cause is worth taking up and how far you would be willing to go on implementing a certain matter before penning it down as a policy.

For an existing policy to remain in your manual, its relevance must be revisited from time to time; if and whenever necessary, the policy must also be reformed.

4. Buy-in of the policy

We all know how significant a role the 'buy-in' of team members plays in the implementation of a policy. If they don't believe in it, they won't do it.

As mentioned above, if multiple stakeholders are involved during policy formulation, more than half the battle is already won. This would help in addressing practical issues which are likely to crop up at the formulation stage.

Moreover, dissenters would know in advance which policies are likely to be non-negotiable. So, when the policy goes live, resistance towards it may be either partly reduced, or better still, completely non-existent. Furthermore, when the team leaders deem something as practical, it does tend to go down better with the rest of the team as well.

While we must attempt to achieve harmony between all concerned stake holders, we know that it isn't always possible. Agendas of a business may on occasion be different from the agendas of its team members.

Let's look at a situation where a company, which is losing money, is forced to gradually lay off some of its team members who are in fact quite competent. In such instances, the reason for such a policy may be shared with the team honestly and its impact on the business explained.

Even the most junior team member would know what choices will be made when a business fails to bear costs beyond a point. This became even more obvious during the pandemic when many restaurateurs found it hard to let go of their trusted solid employees.

In such a situation, an organization is typically trying to balance its concerns about its diminishing reputation as an employer with its need to help counsel its unhappy employees. If you feel it's easy for a person who is being retained to ask another to leave, think again. That person has to do this distasteful job as humanely as possible, while keeping in mind that he could be the next employee to be laid off.

You may recall a lot of businesses during the pandemic had either retained all of their employees at lower salaries or had managed to retain some with their present salaries and laid off the rest. Most teams opted for the former so that the households of all the employees could at least manage their basic expenses until things got better.

5. Repetition

If we look at our own habits—both professional and personal—we are likely to find many that are detrimental to ourselves and others.

At times we make attempts to change our habits… sometimes we succeed, sometimes we fail. At other times, we make no attempt to change them at all, simply declaring them to be human nature and continue to bear the brunt of their impact.

I have found that people successful in breaking old bad habits or creating new ones, don't just have the discipline to do so, but more importantly use repetition to help make the change.

They find ways to repeatedly remind themselves what they need to do and, at times, even get help from people around them by asking others to remind them of what they need to do. Commit to others in your group who have vested interests in making the change happen. Repeated reminders are a wonderful way to ensure that desired changes happen.

In the past few years, I have found that focussed efforts towards these five aspects meet with much better success than anything I previously used. I believe that if you have the patience to work on these aspects, you will agree with me as well. Remember, what you are working towards is not simply developing a rule book that needs to be followed, but, in fact, a system that would gradually transform the way your organization would think, take decisions, solve problems, and work together.

As the renowned novelist and philosopher Ayn Rand once said, "A culture is made—or destroyed—by its articulate voices."

People: The Secret Sauce

It was my first on-the-job training stint at a five-star hotel while studying hotel management, and I was about to get my first lesson on why the food business is called the "people business".

The tick-tock of her heels echoing through the hotel corridors had everyone in the banquet department suddenly standing upright, appearing purposeful, busy and generally scurrying around to put things in the order they are supposed to be. After her inspection—she corrected some staff members, chided some, and, on rare occasions, even complimented a few—the sound of her heels faded and the team finally heaved a collective sigh of relief.

Since then, I have studied people productivity, both supervised and unsupervised, with one singular purpose throughout my career: to understand the impact that mindful presence has on converting a business vision to reality, day after day.

It's tough enough nowadays to attract and retain good talent in the sector. One must also evaluate 'affordability' of people in relation to their performance. An employee, who is 'financially affordable' to the restaurateur, who performs poorly is considered unaffordable, however, an 'expensive' hire who performs well, becomes affordable.

Over the course of time, I have realized that to execute a business vision, my own measure for success in the people department must be how well teams perform in my absence (since I can't always be available), and in the absence of their other leaders, i.e., unsupervised.

While hiring, I look at three things: integrity, attitude, and skill, in that order; because I can teach skills thoroughly, attitude partially, but integrity… not at all.

I find that after screening through these three filters, giving employees what they expect and creating a good work environment usually leads to more engaged employees, thus, more unsupervised productivity and mindful presence.

Some components of a good work environment

- Clear directives: Frequent communication of expectations that are achievable and practical.
- Adequate resources: The best that can be provided to each employee to support their deliverables.
- Rewards and recognitions: For good work performance and initiatives taken, the staff must be acknowledged through announcements, and wherever possible, financially as well.
- Learning and development: Training programs for knowledge building that eventually lead to promotion opportunities.

People: The Secret Sauce

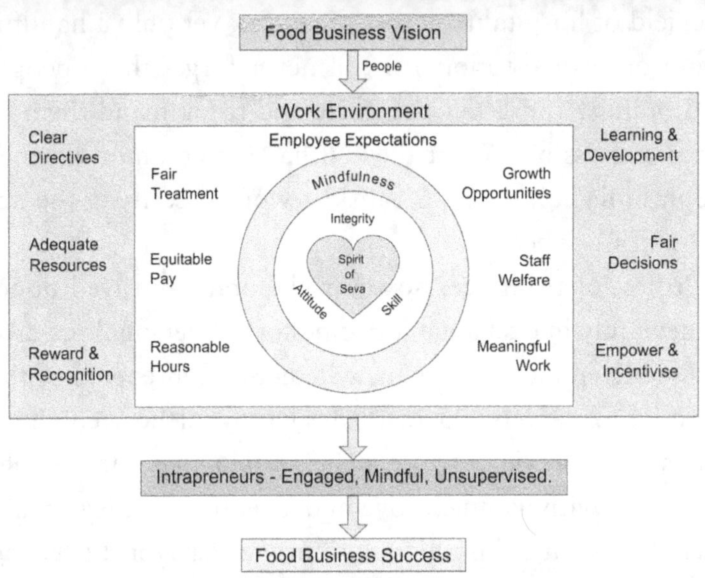

- Fair decisions: Being fair and being 'seen as fair' by the team are both equally critical.
- Empower and incentivize: Encourage each team member to take independent actions that can contribute towards tangible achievement of business goals; offer financial and other incentives to ignite initiative.

An employee who drives the initiatives he is responsible for—both mindfully and unsupervised—is an intrapreneur who can lead his area of the business' vision to reality. Creating many such intrapreneurs contributes greatly towards the success of a business.

For that final edge, you'll need to bring in yet another special ingredient.

The special ingredient of the food industry

I have served and been served by innumerable people in the field of hospitality across the globe, yet only a handful stand out as exceptional. I can never forget those people and brands, and I will patronize and recommend them as often as possible. What they all have in common is what we in India call 'seva', a Sanskrit word describing the act of 'selfless service'.

Professional service, however elaborate and well done, is inevitably in exchange for some sort of personal reward. These incredible individuals, whether entrepreneurs or the most junior servers, throw themselves wholeheartedly into this selfless service. You can be certain that they would serve you with as much love and attention as they would even if they earned nothing in return, except for the feeling of fulfilment that comes from serving others without any ulterior motives.

Now imagine, if some people you hire were to have that true spirit of 'seva' at their core. How much more powerful would your work culture and guest experience be, and what could it do for your business goals?

Ready to find such people for your team, but not sure how? Khalil Gibran has a possible clue– "To understand the heart and mind of a person look not at what he has already achieved, but at what he aspires to."

Managing your team

If you have played the role of an employee in an organization, you will know that a manager runs the establishment while an owner teaches his crew to run it. If you intend to change your role from that of a player to that of a coach, you will need to change your perspective towards certain things first. Remember, coaches don't play the field themselves. They devise a good plan, look for good players, and train them to reach their maximum potential in order to lead the team to victory. Your measure of success would thus change from personal achievement to group performance.

Such practices must be strongly supported by the empowerment of employees to take certain decisions at their own level. One incident that comes to my mind occurred at a small restaurant I visited recently. Being a regular patron on account of their good food, I was once horrified when every single dish they served me and my guests was way below the standards I had come to expect from them. On mentioning this to the supervisor on duty, being the most senior staff member on that shift, he confronted the chef with the leftovers to taste. Besides apologizing profusely and offering to change the meal, he did what few employees at his level could have done independently: he took a call to not charge for the meal. This, in my opinion, was an excellent example of a high level of empowerment and trust existing between an employer and his employees.

A high staff turnover is common in this business. This can disastrously affect your reputation, service and, of course, your restaurant's bottom line. It also results in additional costs in terms of new recruitment and training. We must understand that turnover in itself isn't the problem; it is only a symptom of poor human resource management! Good management entails good recruitment practices backed by a detailed induction program to reduce the learning curve.

Tentative Hierarchy of a Standalone Restaurant

General Manager			
Bar Manager	Bar Tenders	Utility Workers	
Restaurant Manager			
Assistant Manager (front of the house)			
Captains	Stewards	Busboys	
Accountant	Cashiers		
Housekeeper	Cleaners		
Assistant Manager (back of the house)			
Administrative Officer	Telephone Operators	Office Assistants	
Purchase Officer	Stores Clerk		
Personnel Officer			
Property Supervisor	Maintenance Man / Washup Boys		
Chef	Sous Chef	Commis I,II,III	Utility Workers

Ensuring continuous personal and professional employee growth through training opportunities improves employee commitment to your establishment.

What Must Be Explained to Every Employee

Whether an employee is a waiter or a general manager, you will need to brief each team member about your vision for the restaurant and how each of their roles serves that vision.

The better an employee understands his 'birth purpose' in your business, the more likely he is to comply with the directions from his seniors and the more focussed he will be in achieving your vision.

Understanding this at all levels also makes it more natural for junior members to make suggestions and for their seniors to recognize whether those ideas are in the objective interest of your business or not, making for an inclusive and collaborative work culture.

Taking Ownership as an Employee

All employees, regardless of their designation in an organization, need to be accountable and take ownership of their work.

Unfortunately, ownership is often misunderstood… both by the person taking it, and the person expecting it to be taken. We often come across employees who take 'ownership' so literally that they become either high-strung individuals taking biased decisions or self-serving individuals misusing the promoter's resources. Either way, when objectivity is compromised, it is obviously bad for business.

Initially in my career, my need to bond with my team overrode my objectivity in serving the organization. My erstwhile employer, who ran a confectionery chain amongst other businesses, patiently advised me to "be attached and yet detached". I didn't quite understand what he meant then. Many years later, when I took one of the toughest people-related decisions in my work life—firing a colleague—I understood it then.

It so happened that after understanding his problem, I mentored my colleague, covered up for him, and even did some of his work for a certain period of time. At one point, however, when this continued, I realized that if I didn't fire him, I would be doing a disservice to my employer. Personally, I felt terrible when I took that call, but it made me realize just how far a professional had to go to do the right thing, regardless of the unpopularity of such a decision. My need to connect with people is still as strong today as it has always been. Only, I have developed another mechanism within myself which reminds me of the role I have agreed to play for an organization and what it entails. The takeaway here is to be both fair to your business and humane with your team.

To choose a candidate you like or someone who has come through a good reference is good, but objectively try and gauge whether the person will fit the role and serve the business well.

At a basic level, 'taking ownership' simply involves developing and exercising entrepreneurial attitude and abilities within the boundaries of employment.

Managing Your Money

> *"Annual income twenty pounds, annual expenditure nineteen pounds nineteen and six, result happiness. Annual income twenty pounds, annual expenditure twenty pounds ought and six, result misery."*
>
> – Charles Dickens

When viewing your restaurant as a financial entity you will be confronted with issues such as:

- The capital you will invest: how much interest would you have earned if it were your own money parked in a safer investment, and how you will pay back the principal and interest if you have borrowed money for capital.

- Cash flow requirements: whether money coming in is more than the money going out towards expenses and if that payback isn't happening as planned, what you will do.
- Suppliers' credit policy: how soon do you need to pay suppliers to build a healthy relationship with them rather than late payments resulting in supplies being cut off.
- Tracking your financial performance every day, week, and month, and course correcting rather than waiting for unpleasant quarterly findings.

The initial flow of curious customers may fade away leading to a slump or plateau in revenue. Then what?

Resilience at this stage in business is vital to achieving your long-term objectives.

You need to:

- Set realistic budgets and make best and worst case scenario projections.
- Define your accounting policies and procedures.
- Determine the required management information systems.

Whether to lease or buy the property is an important factor. The decision may be one of choice or circumstance. Establishments such as McDonald's often buy the places they run. Buying a property even when prices are low can be a daunting task and entrepreneurs often prefer to lease their premises.

These days, leasing usually works on a 'package' basis with two components: a refundable deposit and a monthly rent. So, a ₹50,000 package could mean a ₹10,00,000 deposit plus ₹40,000 as monthly rent. The interest on the deposit is calculated at the rate of 1% per month i.e., ₹10,000 in this case. Based on the willingness and ability of the landlord and the tenant, the same package may also be worked out as ₹5,00,000 deposit plus ₹45,000 monthly rent.

Furthermore, mutually beneficial payment phases, with a different rent before and after opening, can be negotiated. For example:

- Phase I: Pre-opening rent of ₹30,000 per month.
- Phase II: On opening ₹40,000 per month as a minimum basic amount or 15% of net sales, whichever is higher.

Even so, when deposits are high, it may be advisable to negotiate the proposed property development expenses (immovable assets favouring the landlord's premises) into the deposit. Keep in mind that three years is the conventional benchmark time to breakeven; the duration of the lease should be agreed upon accordingly. Generally, the agreement is signed in multiples of three years, though a few may opt for a longer period (say seven years).

In case of an outright purchase, the purchased property may be used as collateral to procure bank loans for working capital. Lending policies in most cases amount to the maximum extent of 60-75% of the appraised value of the collateral being hypothecated (property, mutual funds, etc.).

While commercial lending rates may range upwards of 12-16%, a personal loan option at a lower rate may be wiser.

Working with a financial entity (such as a bank with whom you have a prior working relationship) can often be leveraged to your advantage. Working on a moratorium arrangement (where payback of the principal amount or monthly rent is postponed for a few months) will ease some of the pressure of the funding process.

Some financial institutions or individuals play the role of venture capitalists and expect equity (a shareholding) in your organization as opposed to recovery of the principal amount plus interest. This kind of arrangement is generally done in large projects. While some degree of your ownership is effectively being given up, the financial acumen of your investor may help you lead your business to fruition.

Buying an Existing Business

Sometimes, an already existing restaurant in an excellent location might not be doing too well. Better management, finance, or different marketing strategies will turn around such a business, and you might be the one who can swing it. This involves assuming responsibility for the existing base of clients, staff, and suppliers that you may alter as you like. Alternatively, your plans for change may not include using these groups and it is only the property that interests you. Based on what you envision, you could negotiate either for the business piecemeal (property, equipment, workforce, goodwill if any!), or as a whole.

Capital Budget

It is a good idea to list out the capital costs your start-up will entail. A broad set of likely components are as follows:

Space-related

- Real estate deposit: A refundable amount deposited with the landlord as security; this amount is often a certain number of times the agreed monthly rent. For e.g., a deposit of six months' rent.
- Civil work: This includes reconstruction, cabling, plumbing, HVAC, drainage, etc. It is usually budgeted at a rate per sq. ft. as agreed upon with the contractor or architect.

Concept-related

Based on the theme, concept, and cuisine of your choice, you can decide on:

- FF&E: Furniture, Fixtures and Equipment. (Movable furniture and heavy equipment, including tables, chairs, sideboards, computers, refrigerators, cooking ranges, coffee machines, microwave ovens, food processors, worktables, storage racks, etc.)
- OS&E: Operating Supplies and Equipment (smallwares, including cutlery, crockery, glassware, linen, silverware, bar tools, kitchen tools, disposables, etc.)
- Brand: Covers one-time design and development costs of creative material, including logo, menu, signages, etc.

Administrative and Compliance-related

Licensing and permissions: One-time costs of trade mark application, company registration, liquor licence, police permission, etc.

Professional fees: One-time costs of recipe creation, architectural fees (e.g., 10% of related project costs such as civil work), legal fees, etc.

Food and Beverage-related

Once you buy your first batch of food and beverage supplies, it serves as your 'opening stock'. Then, keep adding costs of food and beverages as you purchase throughout the month, and on the last day of the month the stock you are left with is called 'closing stock'.

> To know your food cost for the month in rupees, do this:
> Opening Stock + Purchases − Closing Stock = Food Consumed or Food Cost
>
> To know your percentage of Food Cost, simply take:
> Total Sales of the Month / Food Cost

Working capital

Many feel that providing for working capital is unnecessary in a business that sells its products and services for cash. The reality is that from the time you are developing your concept and scouting for your property till you execute your vision and open your restaurant doors to earn your first rupee, your endeavour needs cash. This is the first component of your working capital that must be provided for. This is 'pre-opening' working capital.

The second component of working capital is 'post-opening'. You may not from your first day of opening, hit the sales figures that will allow you to cover your fixed costs of rent, staff, etc. You will need money to cover losses (if any) over the first few months after opening. (Refer to the table on page 117.)

Keeping track

Financial details such as sales (refer to the table on page 118), costs, cash flow, inventories, accounts receivable and payable need to be closely monitored. Alertness on the part of the senior management is critical to a prompt response to any abnormalities such as pilferage.

Studying the Balance Sheet while keeping track of your financial performance through the Profit and Loss account is mandatory. Regular recommendations from your chartered accountant on these matters are useful. A pie chart of the revenue, indicating individual cost components as well as profits, is a good indicator for visualizing any costs threatening to eat into your slice of profit.

Cost Control Tools

The three cost components in a restaurant are food cost, labour cost, and overheads. It is in our best interests to monitor them closely. Devices for their control include:

Food cost

- Manage your supplier rates and terms.
- Manage your inventory of quantities ordered and consumed.

A Sample Working Capital Estimate					
Running Costs	Actual % per month	Actual per month	% during development	₹ during development	Notes
Rent	100%	2,00,000	75%	1,50,000	First month rent free
Staff	100%	2,00,000	50%	1,00,000	Core team hired initially, rest hired on a staggered basis
Utilities	100%	1,00,000	100%	1,00,000	
Marketing	100%	30,000	100%	30,000	For teaser campaign
Miscellaneous	100%	20,000	100%	20,000	
Total		5,50,000		4,00,000	

Component 1: Pre-opening Working Capital: 4 months (projected start-up time) × ₹4,00,000 (running cost during development) = ₹16,00,000

Component 2: Post-opening Working Capital: 3 months (projected time to operational break-even) × ₹5,50,000 (at 100% running cost) = ₹16,50,000

Total Working Capital = ₹16,00,000 (Component 1) + ₹16,50,000 (Component 2) = ₹ 32,50,000, which needs to be added to your capital expenditure.

Restaurant Sales Summary

Date: _________   Time: _________   Cashier: _____________

Check No.	Table No.	Waiter No.	No. of Guests	Restaurant	Bar	Total	Service Charge	Sales Tax	Grand Total	Cash	Credit	Remarks
Total												

Prepared by: _________________   Manager: _________________

- Manage your wastage of raw and cooked food through good processes.
- Use standardize recipes for consistency in costs.

Labour cost

- Keep a candidate evaluation sheet ready with predefined criteria to reduce the likelihood of hiring someone unsuitable.
- Provide a new employee with a job description which specifies their functions and responsibilities.
- Make an orientation checklist to define the schedule for a candidate's induction into the organization in an optimal manner.
- Maintain an attendance and duty roster to monitor workhours and study the labour expense to contribution ratio.
- Conduct training programs and performance appraisal to support an employee's productivity and career progression.
- Have an exit interview to record reasons for leaving, which becomes a reference point for reviewing and revising company policies and practices.

Overhead cost

- Make provision for overhead expenses, including rent, fuel, transport, printing and stationery, advertising and marketing, discounts, etc.
- Professional services hired to help us get people or services of the right calibre.

- Energy-saving procedures and devices can help improve cost effectiveness by reducing consumption of gas, water, and electricity (for example, gas regulators, solar water heaters, etc.).
- An insurance policy which covers the establishment against loss of capital invested in the event of accidents.

Branding, Marketing, and Sales

To attract new customers and make them come back for more, marketing guru Al Ries says it best in one of his videos – "Create a personal brand that tells customers how you are different from your competition and builds your relationship with them daily." He goes as far as to say – "Sales is passé and Advertising is on life support." How then, can we build a brand that resonates with, attracts, and retains customers to a level that we can profit and grow?

Brand development

The objective of brand development is for people to feel that there is no completely satisfactory substitute for your product. A good brand is generally associated with high quality and standards. Innovative design and imaginative management are important factors that help establish your brand to begin with. Once your brand is known and well established, customer loyalty and financial growth follow naturally. Elements of the brand like the name, logo, menu, and all the touch points convey what you and your restaurant brand stand for.

Naming your restaurant

In the name is the identity and exclusivity of your restaurant. Gradually, it will represent what you do and what you stand for.

To find a name you may look at the following areas:

- Use the name of the founder.
- Borrow phrases from music or literature.
- Use words describing the food, service, or ambience you intend to offer.
- Include a particular number, letter of the alphabet, colour, plant, ingredient, etc.
- Utilize an easy-to-pronounce catch word or an easy-to-remember abbreviation, especially in the case of long names.

Logo design

A logo is a symbol which reminds consumers immediately of the company or its product. It should be eye-catching and simple while displaying the ability to influence the consumer. It is instrumental in drawing initial as well as recall attention to the message we are trying to convey.

Menu design

Your menu is a silent salesman and represents the image of your restaurant. The layout must thus be appropriately formatted and sequenced. The first few moments are critical to capturing the patron's attention. The fonts, colours, graphics, and highlighting—all contribute to a well-designed menu.

Marketing

Often, when a story is well told regardless of whether it is true or not, if it resonates with your audience, it can do wonders.

Here's one such story of how perception beats reality…

Many years ago, a rather scruffy man rang my doorbell and thoughtfully suggested I close my windows since they were harvesting honey from the comb on a tree nearby, and the bees might come in.

A while later, he came up with his buddy holding a bucket of wonderful-looking honey with pieces of the honey comb still draining off in it. "Would you like to buy some?" he asked, offering me a stick dripping with it to taste. As I licked if off my finger, I was shocked. It tasted like a cheap sugar syrup cleverly disguised with molasses. Were my taste buds playing tricks on me? This was real pure honey from the tree next door, or so I believed.

So, I asked for another lick and excused myself to my kitchen to wash my hand. As I dropped the 'honey' from my finger into a glass of water, it immediately dissolved instead of dropping to the bottom of the glass as real honey would. This confirmed the fraud I suspected.

I declined the offer, of course, and in the evening asked my neighbours about it. Quite a few had bought it evidently; some of them repeatedly each year. They were convinced by its 'authenticity', with the picture of real bees entering their home and the real honeycomb they saw inside, all at a price slightly lower than the branded bottled honey in the market.

There was no honeycomb nearby and clearly no bees or honey, but when a story is told well (even if it's a lie), perception beats reality! Please know that I am in no way suggesting that you lie about your value proposition, I'm simply sharing this story as an example.

Catering to everyone's needs is difficult and will prove unprofitable. It is best to specifically identify your customer first. In this way you will be able to design your product and service around their requirements. In a coffee shop, for instance, cheery interiors that allow you to conduct meetings, play board games, or work independently on your laptop is a given, while in an up-market restaurant, some kind of entertainment or showmanship may be called for. The public expects such an ambience, enjoys it, and is ready to pay more for it. You have to distinguish between ordering food home and a real dining-out experience. The more you fulfil their expectations, the higher the perceived value of your product.

You first need to identify the consumer segment you intend to serve and create a typical patron profile.

Profile your customer

Multiple profiles of various kinds of guests or patrons you intend to serve could be developed by combining elements from the various factors mentioned below:

Demographics:

Age, sex, marital status, family size, income range, education, occupation, sophistication, ownership of house, car, etc.

Geographic factors:

Urban/suburban, area served, density of population, nature of location (commercial or residential), accessibility, etc.

Psychographics:

Fashion conscious, socially inclined, status seeking, conformist, practical, or fun seeking.

Purchasing patterns:

Based on brand name, location, design, product quality, service, ambience, price, number and type of other clients, packaging, etc.

Market inclinations:

Size, growth rate, direction, changing needs, etc.

Lifestyle factors:

Family, status, media preferences, any significant connections, hobbies, interests, etc.

Research the market

Studying and understanding the habits and preferences of guests helps us be best prepared to serve them. This is where organized market studies like focus group discussions, in-depth interviews, online forms, etc., will give a more accurate picture than just guesswork.

Since this research will be the basis for decision-making all through your implementation, it better be thorough. In short, do your homework well and do it yourself.

Depending on the extent of your knowledge of consumer behaviour and your budget, you could conduct an in-house research study or an outsourced one. Either way, your research should include:

- Understanding existing trends better by talking to targeted consumers, reading, or travelling. For example, while this was being written, Japanese cuisine restaurants and coffee shops with domestically-sourced ingredients was the trend. One could use this information to ride on the crest of the trend wave.

- Observing the competition or similar offers with regards to location, price, product, service, perceived value, product mix, and ambience. While this is often a reflection of consumer preferences, it is often not a comprehensive picture. This is the gap you can fill through points of differentiation or a USP.

Now that you know the various guest profiles you intend to attract, you must figure out the experience you would like them to have.

Curating your guest experience

Once Michelin Star Chef Marco Pierre White said in an interview with regards to guest experience that at any restaurant, it's always your co-diners and ambience that matter first, followed by the service, and finally the food. The reason, as he explained, was that if you are in good company, in a nice place with polite staff, mistakes in food are more easily forgiven. In cloud kitchens these days, if the value for money is good and packaging half decent, even average food seems to be acceptable.

This does not mean you compromise on the quality of food. To deliver a great experience, it is crucial to pay attention to your food, service, ambience, value, presentation, etc., and all the various elements of your brand.

If you manage to get the pulse of the market, people will beat a path to your door.

Deliver the experience

Position yourself right

It's important for your guests to have the right image of your business. If they value friendly service staff or high-society fellow patrons, see how you can give them that. Remember, emphasizing these points differentiates you from the competition.

Price yourself right

There are two ways of looking at pricing:

- **Cost-based:** Determine the cost of raw materials, labour, and overheads. Add your expected margin of profit to achieve your selling price. The standard rule of thumb is to estimate profit to be one-third of your selling price. Obviously, this cannot be blindly applied to all items on the menu. The margins on different items vary, but average out at a certain ratio. This rule of thumb helps you keep costs in perspective.
- **Market-based:** Determine market acceptability in terms of the perceived value for money that clients

get from your competitors. If your actual costs are more than those of your competitors, your selling price would have to be higher.

Pricing is a tricky decision and a mistake in this area means certain failure.

Your mission statement

A mission statement is a concise summary of your restaurant's goals and business philosophy. It helps your team understand the values and behaviour expected over the long term. If it is made public, it also allows your customers to better understand your brand. You can define your mission statement based on:

- Scope of work
- Business philosophy
- Public perception
- Industry perception
- Management style
- Attitude towards guests or patrons
- Financial objectives
- Standards in food, service, ambience, and price

More marketing

To better position your restaurant, it is a good practice to list your Strengths, Weaknesses, Opportunities and Threats (S.W.O.T.) at regular intervals. Feedback from mystery diners provides a valuable insight into your business from an outsider's viewpoint. It's wonderful if the reports are good, and if not, you have something to work on. Specific criteria for evaluation must be defined, such as friendliness, personal appearance, job knowledge, time balance (quick service without making the guest feel hurried), etc.

Guest Feedback Forms are hardly ever read or acted upon. Once a restaurant is running smoothly, such activities become low priority and the forms are inevitably filed away. The fact is that even a simply-designed form provides enough information to make a difference.

I was delighted when one suburban restaurant actually called me on my anniversary, thanked me for my patronage and informed me of a food festival that was on. You can be sure I went back soon for more and with friends, too. These restaurateurs realized that I chose to visit them over all the other options that I had and understood the value of the repeat business that I gave them. You have only one chance to make a good impression and that determines whether your guest will return.

Defining customized procedures for guest greeting, farewell, telephone enquiries, or service is a useful practice. You must ensure that over-friendliness does not encroach on the privacy that the guest may be seeking. Remember that the days of standardized selling, where all waiters at any point in time are recommending exactly the same dishes to all guests, are long gone. Making recommendations should be a natural process where suggested dishes are the preferred choice of the individual serving them. Guests these days know the difference between standardized restaurant selling and truly personalized recommendations. It is critical that listening for specific clues to the guest's preference becomes a habit so that recommendations do not starkly differ from the expectations with which the guest walked into your restaurant.

Some restaurateurs still encourage their staff to practise aggressive selling techniques in order to increase the average bill per head. Such methods may succeed in increasing sales for a short period but it will eventually tire patrons. Instead, try to interest them enough to refer your restaurant to others and make them return for more.

Whenever you hear people talking excitedly about a particular restaurant, notice how they don't just say a place is good 'generally'. Patrons are discerning enough to talk specifics–"They barbecue their starters on a live coal grill set in your table; you can actually buy the furniture you sit on in their restaurant; it's the perfect place to connect with other artists…"

Proactively offering 'something different' gives guests specifics to talk about—the path to getting referred business.

To keep your business 'lively', you have to infuse new life into it by way of décor, events, menu, etc., every couple of weeks or months. Patrons tire of the novelty of a new idea quite quickly, and are constantly in search of innovations on offer. Every few years, even the most avant-garde restaurant needs a facelift.

Where to find information

- Competitors
- Trade associations
- Trade magazines
- Trade schools

- Trade suppliers
- Government offices
- Libraries, websites, directories
- Surveys through professional agencies or student interns
- Yellow pages
- Entrepreneurial biographies

Marketing activities you could initiate

- Plan a marketing calendar with a professional PR firm or advertising agency.
- Organize a contest or treasure hunt with a 'dinner for two' prize for the winners.
- Support your neighbourhood by sponsoring landscape maintenance or other causes they value.
- Get a celebrity to cook their favourite dishes at your restaurant.
- Organize a wine or beer festival at your restaurant sponsored by liquor brands interested in earning brownie points with their end-users who are your patrons. Another popular item on the list is wine by the glass—usually a brand not easily available in the outside market.
- Offer a discount for Happy Hours. Something for free will always be appreciated and a complimentary dish or drink builds up a reasonable amount of goodwill. However, the cost of offering such discounts should be regularly measured and controlled. Caution must be exercised when offering these discounts in an upscale restaurant and some level of discretion

is critical to the feel-good factor of these offers. Being too blatant may make more affluent clients uncomfortable when entertaining their guests.

- Design memorabilia: calendars, mugs, pens, notepads, t-shirts, stickers, etc.
- An art display, flea market or other such bazaar inside your premises may create a sense of liveliness and association amongst patrons.
- Ask your chef to create a special 'tasting menu' with a platter of colourful and varied bite-sized morsels and let patrons know through a tie-up with a radio channel, credit card, or mobile phone company. Signature dishes or drinks creatively designed with the cost-effective ingenuity of the chef or bar manager add a distinctive touch to the menu.
- Design attractive stationery: menu, logo, brochures, visiting cards, letterheads, etc.
- Use follow-up stationery: thank-you letters, anniversary greetings, birthday and suggestion cards.
- Participate in industry seminars either educationally or financially.
- Invite guest chefs for their appraisal of specialities that can be publicized in the media. An in-house cookery class for amateurs conducted by your chef would enhance public approval and a participatory spirit. The event may be sponsored by vendors of specialized ingredients or equipment who may promote or sell their products there.
- Create a Facebook and Instagram page to alert patrons about the happenings at your restaurant.

- Sponsor a charity or cultural event or participate at a community festival. On such an occasion, offer one interesting dish at an astonishingly low price. For e.g., a softy at McDonald's sold for ₹20. The individual profit on this item is irrelevant. It is the driving in of more sales and goodwill that matters. Be sure not to run out of this item or your guests will get really upset.
- Boost the experience your guests have at your restaurant by engaging a live entertainer such as a musician, stand-up comedian, or other performer to entertain them.

These activities need to be thought out for the opening phase as well as during ongoing operation of the restaurant. Their costs could either be borne by your own organization or in some cases by co-sponsors in exchange for visibility of their brand in a desirable location.

Your online presence could include:

- An interesting history of your restaurant
- A colourful menu with photographs where possible
- Happening visitors and events
- Job opportunities
- FAQs and memorabilia, if any

Avenues that may be pursued

Technology:

Handheld POS (Point of Sale) systems are an option in restaurants these days. This eliminates the manual clumsiness of illegible handwriting, waiting in line at the area terminal to punch in information, and time spent in walking to the kitchen. The guest is never left unattended and the number of service employees required is decreased.

Retail:

This involves developing one or more products on your menu to make them shelf-friendly and available for consumers to purchase at local supermarkets. For instance, a Bangalore-based restaurant chain Nagarjuna, well-known for its delicious biryani, neatly packages this food item and sells it to consumers at local shopping malls.

Outsourcing:

Restaurants may outsource their housekeeping or valet services and even a few dishes such as desserts, for example. They may also hire external services for their laundry, filing of tax returns, and managing their payroll, website, etc. Rather than undertaking the time, cost, and effort of creating an infrastructure for such services or products themselves, getting them from elsewhere may actually be more practical (though more expensive) in some instances.

Competitive advantage

Every organization differentiates itself from others by its offer in terms of values, people, and product mix. Having a sustainable differentiation would mean that a competitor cannot easily replicate your offer. While there may be many imitators of a good concept, if their offer is not deeply rooted in values, it will ultimately be a superficial replica without the core essence that is fundamental to any brand.

You may choose to offer something either extremely uncommon, or something that's quite common but done differently. Either way, it is important to plan right down to the last detail.

Success is inevitably in the execution, and execution can only happen through people. Thus, investing yourself in the engagement and retention of good people (staff) is possibly the most critical foundation. Incentives like sweat equity, a percentage of profit, shorter work days or work weeks, consultancy status that increases the employee's take-home salary (while reducing the employer's Cost to Company), etc., work well in bringing consistent excellence to the business.

The product mix is yet another point of differentiation through which you can wow your patron. This decision will stem from which patron groups you intend to attract and your judgement of how to uniquely appeal to their imagination. For instance, you may have a distinctive dish with your own inimitable spice blend that even your chefs, if poached by a competitor, cannot replicate.

Observing consumers and understanding their habits will help you define the social purpose of your brand. So, for instance, if your social stance is 'coffee and conversations', consumers know what to expect and will go out and seek this from your brand. The closer the delivery of this experience is to their expectations, the more they will see your brand promise being fulfilled. This directly translates into effectively influencing their buying habits and thus patronage in your favour.

It may also be helpful to learn from other retail sectors. Their best practices include areas such as: technologically supported metrics, supply chain management and visual merchandizing that may help improve the measurement of performance gaps, management of inventory, optimization of product presentation, etc. So, studying the way a department store merchandizes its products may be useful in presentation at our restaurant deli. Or, the way a multiplex measures its seat occupancy per show and shows per day may be applied to our chair occupancy per sitting and number of lunch and dinner sittings per day.

Successful projects usually have a strong leadership and well-articulated vision backed by a clear business strategy.

The strategic action plan for a restaurant should consider the following initiatives:

- Develop your team members' skills and knowledge over time.
- Innovate, so your competition can't easily copy you.
- Strategically tie-up or co-brand with allied businesses.
- Frequently review all management functional activities (marketing, finance, HR, operations, R&D, supply chain, and manufacturing).
- Investigate brand extension in terms of diversification and geographic consumer coverage.

Sales forecasting

The primary factors affecting restaurant sales include:

- Demand for the concept
- Characteristics of that particular site

- Price to Portion size ratio
- Competition
- Quality of management
- Advertising and promotions
- Unexpected natural calamities (the biggest one being the pandemic)

Thus, the accuracy of sales forecasting depends on our ability to define and measure these variables. You need to organize and analyze information in a way that makes it possible to estimate what kind of sales you will generate. Decisions on the intended target audience, specific product mix, daily-expected number of guests, average bill per head, etc., can help you get a fix on these projections.

Firstly, you need to create different customer segments. For example, those that visit on weekdays, weekends, lunch, and dinner. For each segment you need to tabulate:

> Number of guests × Average check = Total sales
> Average check is the amount each guest spends at your restaurant (Average check = Total sales / Number of guests)

To maximize your potential in restaurant sales, it is necessary to maximize your use of resources.

Your restaurant has a fixed number of seats. Obviously, the higher the number of times guests occupy seats each day, the higher your sales will be. For example, if you have a 100 cover restaurant and serve 150 meals over lunch and dinner, your seat turnover ratio will be 1.5.

> Seat turnover ratio = Meals served / Cover capacity
> (i.e. = 150 / 100 = 1.5)

A 1.5 ratio is all right; more is excellent, while less may not be economically viable.

Staff can be more effectively utilized by offering additional services using the existing infrastructure:

- Banquet services (on- or off-premises)–depending on the kitchen capacity and the availability of dining space.
- Parcel deliveries–depending on the kitchen capacity and the promoter's stance of whether to use aggregator's staff, or own staff, or both, for delivery.

Bringing in sales

There are only three ways to increase your revenues:

1. Increasing the number of people patronizing your organization.
2. Increasing the frequency of patronage from your guests.
3. Increasing the average expenditure per person.

Once you have identified target segments of customers, you need to review factors that may be limiting you. They may exist in terms of your menu, concept, location, parking space, number of covers, or skill level of staff. You need to keep reviewing these factors to maximize their potential contribution.

Selling through aggregators and other platforms

Like Amazon is an aggregator platform where consumers can simultaneously buy many products from many sellers, similarly, in the restaurant and food industry, there are aggregators who connect hungry consumers with loads of eateries they can consider buying from.

So, aggregators in the restaurant industry connect buyers with sellers. They offer buyers a range of restaurants, cuisines, and dishes to choose from based on their location. Customers can see the delivery time, price, etc., of the dishes they would like to order and make an informed choice.

What aggregators offer restaurateurs is:

a) Online menu presence: For which restaurateurs pay aggregators a percentage of their sales (usually 25% or above).

`b) Discovery: For new restaurants to be discovered and show up high on the list of options, restaurateurs can choose from various marketing packages by paying either a flat fee per month or a per-click fee or by offering discount schemes to their customers.

c) Delivery: Aggregators arrange for a pick-up from the restaurant and delivery to the customer for which the customer pays a fee.

d) Billing and payment collection: The aggregator provides the customer with various easy payment options in the app. They collect payments and later pay the restaurant the sales amount minus their aggregator commission.

Different aggregators and platforms offer different combinations of the above services.

Aggregators like Swiggy and Zomato, for instance, offer all the above services. They see themselves at the centre of the ecosystem of buyers and sellers, and since they bring in the customers, they do not share customer details with restaurateurs.

A platform like Dunzo offers only a delivery service at a certain rate per kilometre.

A platform like Thrive does not offer discovery but offers all the other above-mentioned services. It offers its services for a percentage fee and its delivery service—being a tie-up with delivery agencies like Dunzo or WeFast—is transparent about the delivery charge rates per kilometre.

Platforms like Dunzo, WeFast, and Thrive see themselves as service providers to restaurateurs and customers, and since restaurateurs bring in the customers themselves, they are aware of the details of their clients.

For restaurateurs to understand decision-making on selling through aggregators like Swiggy and Zomato, it is important to recall their history with restaurants. When aggregators first entered the market, they pitched two solutions to restaurateur problems.

One, that they would offer a reliable and economical delivery network, considering that delivery boys and their vehicles were expensive and hard for restaurateurs to maintain.

Two, that they would increase restaurant sales by encouraging new customers to discover our brand and remind old ones of our presence through their app.

Initially, it worked well for everyone, especially start-ups, as aggregator commissions were affordable to restaurateurs at the time and customers got multiple choices from where they could order instantly. Gradually, new challenges began cropping up. Aggregators frequently asked for higher commissions to serve their investors. Only those restaurant brands that could afford the expensive advertising packages or discount packages for the aggregators showed up at the top of search results. Aggregators refused to share customer information; they offered such deep discounts to the customers that even the restaurateurs who created those very dishes couldn't afford to sell them at those prices. They even tried running their own kitchens using the data they had gathered from restaurant deliveries.

Working with aggregators had become unaffordable, and more importantly, unfair. Several large restaurant chains and restaurant associations opposed these practices and even appealed to the government for intervention. By this time, however, aggregators had succeeded in habituating customers to ordering through their app and this put the restaurant industry in jeopardy.

Subsequently, start-up restaurateurs realized that it would be best to create their own brand identity strong enough for customers to distinguish their brand from others in the crowd independent of aggregators. For a few months initially, some start-ups may even undertake the aggregators' advertising or discount packages, but soon realize that the eventual price they pay to stay on top of that list just isn't worth it.

Many restaurant brands have their own delivery network in addition to that of the aggregators and offer their customers a better price to order from them directly.

The aggregators are an undeniable part of the restaurant ecosystem and, over the years, restaurateurs have rather painfully learnt how to deal with them. Recently I have heard that a few aggregators have begun selectively sharing some customer information, especially with larger restaurant chains, so there is hope for a more amicable future.

Is social media really the holy grail of marketing?

Whenever we hear of a new restaurant, like anything else that's new, we look it up on Google. So, it is quite true that a restaurant that isn't visible online usually doesn't exist in the minds of customers.

A website, no matter how basic, can be considered the 'hub' of our online presence and platforms like Instagram or Facebook our 'spokes'. The premise is that a potential customer (new or existing), who discovers interesting photographs, written content, or other engaging news about the brand, is more likely to buy from it.

Social media companies help you create and traverse these paths of online communication with a view to bring in leads which hopefully convert to sales.

Customers first become aware of your restaurant (through reliable word of mouth sources or by looking at online reviews), only then they may engage with your brand and consider buying from it, and, then finally... buy. That's how you make a sale.

I find social media to be a great tool for brand awareness; it often serves as a reminder of your existence. It may even lead to engagement and customer interactions, however, unless you provide a direct link to make an immediate purchase (through your website or an aggregator), it rarely leads to a dine-in purchase. Once out of sight, it goes out of mind, like the numerous brands we are bombarded with during our online explorations.

So, a presence on social media has now become a sort of 'fear of missing out' necessity.

Revenue management

With the wide variety of dining options available to a customer nowadays, it is becoming increasingly difficult to attract 'enough' footfalls from new or existing patrons. Marketing exercises may prove expensive, particularly for smaller enterprises, while sales exercises might even be detrimental. In fact, the more bombarded consumers are with sales offers, the more they can sense even the most subtle sales pitch, and the more likely they are to resist it with a vengeance. Therefore, all efforts towards increasing the footfall and retaining the customer must additionally be supported by managing price, capacity, and time based on demand. This is where management of revenue can help.

Simply put, Revenue Management (RM) is the process of understanding, anticipating, and reacting to consumer behaviour in order to maximize revenue. This concept has been in use for a long time, starting with airlines, followed by hotels, restaurants, and a number of other businesses. Earlier, for instance, an airline seat was sold at a fixed price, whereas now it is priced differentially. Such decisions are based on differential customer demand supported by criteria such as flight timing, routing, days of the week, etc. It is important that the customer sees this differential pricing as fair. For example, a passenger may see no problem paying full fare if he has arrived at the last minute, even if he knows that his neighbour's seat may have been sold at a far lower rate on account of it being booked 30 days in advance.

In restaurants more specifically, RM is about selling covers/seats at the right price to the right customer at the right time.

One of the foremost authorities on the subject is Sheryl E. Kimes of The Center for Hospitality Research, Cornell University. The concept she has developed for restaurants is referred to as revPASH (Revenue Per Available Seat Hour).

In general,
Restaurant Sales = Average Check x Footfalls for the Day

In Revenue Management,
Restaurant Sales = Level of Seat Capacity Utilization x Revenue Per Available Seat Hour (hours that meals are offered).

For example, if the sales for a three-hour lunch shift is ₹96,000 and you have 80 covers, your revPASH would be:

₹96,000 / (3 x 80) = ₹400.

So, each available seat can potentially earn ₹400 per hour during lunch.

The best starting point is to create one-hourly periods of your meal hours for all days of the week. Then, study and note the typical occupancy during these periods based on historic observation, i.e., the extent of empty seats per hour. Imagine and recognize the potential had they all been full in all periods of the day and week. Realistically, since this rarely happens, one needs to ask oneself: given my operating constraints, who is the right person to buy my product or a variation of it during these lean hours, and what might he be willing to pay for it? The answer to this will be opportunities to consider and implement.

For this, one needs to initiate:

1. Demand-based pricing: This involves segmenting the market into various types of customers/potential customers, and deciding what price might attract which customer type at what time during underutilized periods (low demand hours). It is important that this is achieved without the guest perceiving it as unfair, as in the airline example above. In the case of restaurants, an example of a fair differential price offer could be an economically-priced executive lunch while dinner pricing remains marginally higher.

2. Duration management: This entails containing the duration of the customer's meal time without compromising on their experience. Such an exercise requires considering uncertainties like the time when the guest will arrive, the time he will spend at the table and the time between one guest leaving and the next arriving at the table. Each of these time periods must be considered independently to find out apt solutions.

3. Some considerations for decision-making on differential pricing and meal duration are:

a) Table Reservations Policy: For example, some restaurants offer a choice of two meal sittings on weekend nights when accepting reservations. Through this policy they are conveying to their guests that 'an experience of two hours at our restaurant will cost you so much'. They are further ensuring a minimum of two full table turn-arounds with the possibility of more. What they are doing is effectively managing both meal duration and guest arrivals.

b) Table Configuration: One restaurant wanting to attract groups of six to eight people decided on having most of their seating capacity supported by large tables of this size. On starting the restaurant, they discovered that while one part of their client base was indeed groups of this size, around half their patrons came in groups of two to four. As a result, during peak hours, new guests waited in line while noticing that several eight-seater tables were either nearly empty or occupied by only two to four people. Rather than identifying this as a problem, the restaurant management took pride in preserving the sanctity of the experience for their seated guests while simultaneously making their restaurant more aspirational by having new guests wait. The truth is, had they perceived this as a problem and done a cost-benefit analysis, they would have realized that the cost of reconfiguring the restaurant with a table mix better suited to their client base would have cost them less than one month's earnings. As a result, they could have not only increased their revenue but also made their guests happier with less waiting time. Besides, a full restaurant would certainly be far more aspirational than a less crowded one.

c)   On the other hand, keeping small and combinable tables is not a feasible solution either as this may pose a similar problem. For instance, when a large group visits your restaurant, they will have to wait until the required number of adjoining tables are vacated. Thus, to have a few large tables, specifically designated for larger groups, becomes necessary. Judgement calls would need to be made on a case-by-case basis as the guests arrive about which group should be seated first and how.

d)   Table Allocation Policy: Guests, nowadays, mainly prefer being seated on a first-come-first-serve basis on arrival (despite table reservations in advance). They have come around to accepting a policy that allocates a table to a group who came in after them, provided the group's size corresponds with the earliest vacated table more aptly than their own. Then again, when celebrities are allowed to skip the line, most guests resent it, though only a few complain and even fewer demand that they be served first. One must consider the sentiments of their patrons when making such policies.

e) Service Response Time: Obviously, it is critical that the sanctity of guest experience is not compromised while reducing the wait time. You will find that the central part of the guests' meal like main course, dessert, etc., is where they like to linger and enjoy their experience the most. Thus, not rushing them during this period is most important. On the other hand, when guests ask for the check, it is most likely an indication of wanting to end their experience and move on to something else they have in mind, so urgency in presenting the check will suit both: you and the guests. Likewise, the first order of the guests is an indication of their need to commence the experience and they are unlikely to take offence if they are served fairly quickly. They may, in fact, even be hungry and want the service to be deliberately expedited. Again, a quick pace at this point will suit you both. So, service time can be easily quickened during two periods: the time between which guests order their first drink/dish until the time it is served, and the time between which the guests ask for the check until it is presented. Our control is limited in the period between which they place the second and subsequent orders until they ask for the check. Managing this time period would require much more adept sensing and handling on the part of the service staff.

f) Restaurant's 100% Seating Capacity: While most restaurants pack in maximum seating in the design stage itself, certain scenarios may lend themselves to increase capacity to over 100%. For example, a special party where either a stand-up buffet with partial seating or laid-out additional seats may be acceptable to the guest as not compromising on the experience. Typically, the cost of pulling this off is just some additional temporary staff that augments your existing team for the occasion.

g) Operating Style: The way the front or back of the house operates also has an impact on the time your guests will spend at the table. Some styles of kitchen operation such as assembly-line menus offering pre-plated food, or, service styles implemented in cafeterias—where self-service is encouraged—naturally lend themselves to a quick table turnover. One may consider reconstructing some of these when attempting to enhance productivity of your restaurant's underutilized capacity.

A restaurateur may identify and use numerous considerations to further their revenue management goals. Some RM practitioners adopt certain tactics simply because they have seen others use them successfully. The ones who have a deeper understanding of this concept have a greater edge as they can innovate and discover new ways as they go along, rather than blindly follow others.

Revenue management is not intended to replace other tools of sales enhancement such as employee productivity, customer relationship management, etc. Instead, it must be used in conjunction with them to develop a holistic continuous-improvement model. I have found RM to be useful during start-ups, essential during development, and critical during turnarounds.

Managing Your Guests

"We cannot always oblige; but we can always speak obligingly"
— Voltaire

Customer experience, customer care, consumer centricity are buzz words for entrepreneurs in most industries around the globe—a new cause for businesses to work towards. After all, isn't it worth spending time thinking about the patronage of the one person, the customer, also known as king/god in our business? So, customers are, in fact, not an interruption of your work as a restaurateur, but the reason you have work.

In today's competitive market, every brand in business is trying to topple other brands by first identifying customer needs and then bragging about how they understand the customer better. Businesses take a variety of initiatives to enhance customer experience with the intention of acquiring new customers and retaining existing ones. Which of these actually contribute towards an improvement in customer experience is something every brand manager, business head, or owner needs to ask themselves.

Is it only food, service, and ambience or is there something more?

Let's start with the flow of customer influence...

The Flow of Customer Influence

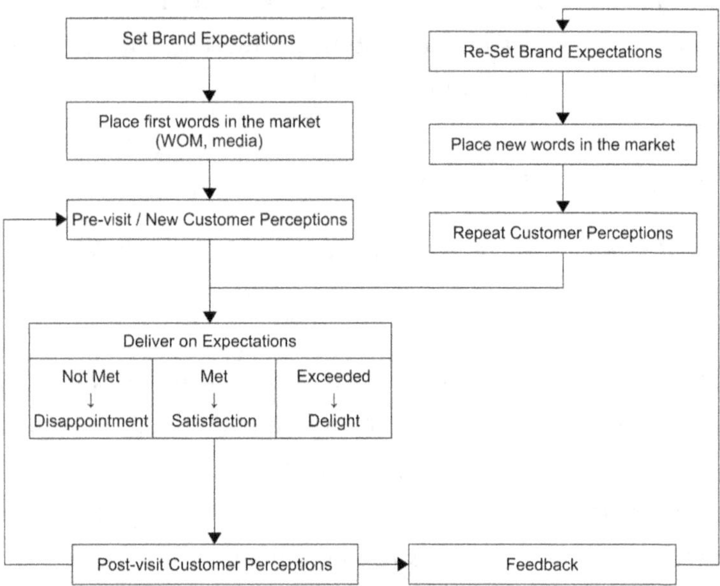

Considering and managing these aspects of customer influence can favourably influence the outcome of your business.

Set your brand expectations

What would you ideally want people to say about your restaurant when it is new and doesn't carry the legacy of history that an existing restaurant does?

What you have envisioned as your brand delivery to your customer in terms of value proposition and what your brand stands for becomes the customer's expectations. Once you have defined this internally, it is entirely up to you to decide how to convey this to your target audience.

Well-planned communications will help you set customer expectations closest to where you want them to be, at least until the first time they visit, after which they will develop their own inferences about your brand. These inferences may or may not be consistent with what you have planned or communicated.

An effort towards making your guests enjoy their experience at your restaurant is the key. You may, for instance, charm your guests by entertaining them with a live performer, or, engage kids with video games while they await their meal. Regardless of whether you are appreciated, such efforts will rarely go unnoticed.

Your first communication in the market

If we hear good things about a particular restaurant, it stimulates our curiosity enough to consider an initial visit. We usually hear about restaurants for the first time from our family, friends, or associates who convey their impressions to us through word of mouth, or, we may learn about restaurants though the media. As it happens, we are more likely to trust someone we know rather than a paid-for piece of communication. Still, we do get influenced by the media.

We may also hear of a new restaurant when we have been invited by someone to visit it—either the promoters themselves or someone who has heard about it before we have.

So, leveraging word of mouth and the media effectively and economically through people you know will help influence new customers to patronize your restaurant. This will lead to pre-visit perceptions or new customer perceptions.

Deliver on expectations

Now, it's time to deliver on your brand promise, consistent with what your guests expect.

The greatest challenge is to achieve customer delight with every guest, every day, on the telephone and on the restaurant floor... one interaction at a time. Remember that at your restaurant, at any given point in time, all your guests will have different experiences with every member of your team.

Post-visit customer perceptions

Once customers have visited your restaurant and availed of the experience, two things happen:

a) They will decide whether or not to patronize your brand again, and, if so, whether with gusto or only to give it another chance.

b) They will convey their feedback to 'new customers'. This will determine whether or not new customers will perceive your brand favourably and visit it as well.

For a healthy business, it is absolutely essential to have a strong base of repeat patrons frequenting your restaurant and speaking about it favourably to others. So, the importance of good delivery cannot be understated.

Guest feedback and its importance

Your customer's feedback about their experience at your restaurant is invaluable in bridging gaps between your brand promise and actual delivery. Listening to your customer constantly and tweaking your brand offer accordingly is the best way to build a business that is aligned to the marketplace. The way to collect such data is naturally through the people who are in direct contact with the guests—your employees, who are your eyes and ears in the field.

The best feedback is usually through a direct conversation. The next best is through a 'Guest Comment Card'. Unfortunately, cards with negative comments, particularly about the team that has served your guests, may not always reach you. Many restaurateurs try to bridge this gap by using a serial number on every card. Some even offer their own mobile phone number for direct access. Of course, a disappointed guest may not have the inclination to fill up such a card when upset or when their server is implicated may not be encouraged by the staff to document their complaint. Should your employees suggest ideas that will strengthen your business, they should be rewarded.

Ensure that you try and get feedback from at least one guest at each table in your restaurant.

Often guests don't offer feedback till they are asked. You might be missing out on valuable insights if your team is not oriented towards asking for feedback. Sometimes guests may be unwilling to share their feedback even if asked, particularly when they are upset.

While the guests are at your premises, it is crucial to try and learn about their experience and get them to share their suggestions and disappointments, as once they leave, you most likely have lost that opportunity forever. Incentivize your guests if necessary and promptly make it up to them if you have learnt of a lapse on the part of your brand.

When confronted with an angry or dissatisfied guest, simply giving them a discount is useless. If you want them to return, it is advisable to approach the issue with sensitivity. Listen to their issue and quickly apologize for their bad experience. Then, investigate the matter, resolve it, thank them for bringing it to your attention, and request the opportunity to serve them again.

Do not argue with your guest or take things personally or quote company policies. A personal prejudice or bias may hamper objective decision-making and self-surveillance is called for. Train your employees to do the same.

One cannot adequately emphasize the importance of a smile. Genuine warmth cannot be taught, but its cultivation can certainly be encouraged. Knowing what your guests love about your brand will help you understand what to build on and what to use as a selling point.

Even more important is what you do with negative feedback from your guests. Some experienced restaurateurs have pointed out that there are times when guests give negative feedback only to get freebies and this is true. But once you know that the complaint is genuine, don't hesitate to accept your mistake, apologize (which is sometimes hard to do), and correct it or make good the experience the best that you can.

If many guests are complaining about the same issue, you either need to change it or attempt to alter that aspect of their expectation altogether. There are occasions when just one guest can give you an insight that can alter the course of your business for the better. Crediting guests with changes—instituted at their behest—gives them a sense of ownership of your restaurant and is known to forge deep promoter-customer relationships and associations with your brand like nothing else.

Other ways to measure brand experience

I have found an anonymous audit of your brand experience from your guests' perspective to be a worthwhile exercise. Mystery dining or an incognito brand audit is a useful tool. This involves first listing out all aspects of your brand promise in terms of food, service, ambience, etc. Next, each aspect must be given a certain priority and weight. Let's say you have decided that 'Service Staff Presentation' is an aspect that holds eight points out of your total score of 100 for your entire restaurant experience. Within this aspect, for instance, you may allocate three points for staff disposition, three for grooming and two points for uniform. Based on their experience, your mystery diner will rate each of these aspects and sub-aspects out of their respective maximum scores, thereby giving you an insight into what is truly happening at your restaurant.

The right customer experience

Meaningful customer experiences are:

- Memorable
- Emotionally-engaging
- Purposeful
- Consistent

Let's get back to basics for a moment.

Before 'hospitality' (the term as we know it today) became a commercial industry, it was initially practised in the private domain by extending a warm welcome to the guests who visited our homes.

Try and recall some of the most memorable meals or house guest experiences you have had either at your own home or someone else's.

A few things are definite:

- We feel good when we are welcomed or served by others, and, often when we serve others as well.
- We remember good food and rave about it.
- We remember hospitable hosts and the wonderful times we had.
- When both the food and the company (hosts and other guests) are good, it makes for a memorable moment in our lives.
- If either the food or the company is bad, the occasion becomes memorable for the wrong reasons.
- Lastly, even if the food is average but the company is good, it will still be a good and genuine moment. However, if the food is excellent but the company

is only average, it may be a good moment but its genuineness will certainly be questionable.

Replicating a genuine home hospitality experience in a commercial setting is obviously not easy. However, if genuineness of experience is what we endeavour to achieve in our offer, then from the above scenarios, it is obvious that it is the 'people element' that is crucial to realizing a positively memorable experience. While people certainly include our guests that directly contribute to the ambience, it is in fact our employees who serve the customers that are key to delivering our brand promise.

Rather than simply expect our employees to love our customers, given the motivation that no customer is equal to no salary, we must consider the fact that an employee in our industry spends more time at his workplace than at his home. Surely, we can spend a reasonable amount of time and money on our employees—also known as our internal customers.

- Like the customers, employees want to believe in a brand and the people behind it.
- As a customer buys into experiences leading to brand loyalty, so does an employee.
- As a customer is nurtured through recognition and engagement, so is an employee.
- As we act upon consumer needs and wants for their loyalty, so must we for employees.
- Just like we develop communications and rewards in sync with our customer profile, we can develop them for our employees.

- As for a customer, each successive positive brand experience builds satisfaction over time, so does it for an employee.
- Just as customers want a good experience before and after the purchase, so do employees who are going to join or have just joined an organization.
- Much like customers and employers expect their needs to be consistently delivered and exceeded, so do employees.
- As customers and employers put up with employee's mistakes, employee's put up with mistakes that their customers and employers make.

If you ignore the need to look after your employees, you will slowly have a team of passively loyal employees. This means people who continue coming to work every day while being too lazy to be productive or lacking the confidence to move to other jobs. This group of people is most dangerous to the organization and they require special focus as they inevitably influence the rest of team.

As we know, Standard Operating Procedures are necessary guidelines created to facilitate a consistent delivery in customer experience time after time. Yet, when employees of an organization deliver rehearsed lines to a customer, they are delivering a somewhat superficial customer experience. When they are empowered to delight the customer with spontaneous acts of kindness they are more likely to deliver excellence in customer service.

Remember that genuine customer experience is not only the responsibility of the brand manager or the business head. Every single person associated with the brand—employees, customers, and even vendors—are a part of the experience. There is no shortcut to building strong relationships and earning people's trust. Genuine caring about the needs of each of these groups and then developing a model that allows synergic interaction between each group is the best... possibly the only way forward to delivering genuine customer experience.

Managing Food Safely

"An ounce of prevention is worth a pound of cure."
– Benjamin Franklin

Food safety is all about producing food safely. After all, any paying customer rightfully expects that food handled by professionals in a restaurant will at least be as well managed as food handled at home. To protect public health, the government outlines certain standards for food safety and audits food establishments to ensure that those safety standards are met. Yet many restaurateurs look at food safety as desirable but not a necessary element in a restaurant. Those unaware of its criticality to their business unfortunately follow such practices merely for the sake of legal adherence, rather than for their real worth.

While getting into trouble with the food safety authorities for poor practices or facing lawsuits from consumers are good enough reasons to address this issue, practising it instead as a moral obligation to the society we serve and to ensure the safety of our patrons is a far healthier premise.

Allowing food to get contaminated, either on account of lack of knowledge of its handling or sheer negligence, is an act of highest carelessness a restaurateur can exhibit toward their patrons.

Ask yourself: What is the use of the tastiest food if it isn't safe to eat?

Understanding and undertaking responsibility for the safe handling of food from the time you purchase it till the time your guest consumes it is, therefore, the most basic of consumer expectations. If you think that the cost of initiating and maintaining food safety standards is high, I'd like to assure you that the cost of not doing so is considerably higher. Responsibly assuring public safety is a given. It has a direct bearing on your reputation, sales, profits, and your relationships all around.

Food poisoning is an acute illness caused by the contamination of food. Adulterants may be biological, such as Salmonella bacteria from improperly cleaned food or a virus from sewage-polluted water; chemical, though contaminants like lead; or even natural toxins like those present in certain mushrooms.

The human body naturally reacts to such contaminants by trying to eject them from the system by vomiting or diarrhoea. Stomach pain and fever typically accompany these symptoms. While in most cases of food poisoning, healthy adults usually recover within a week, in extreme cases, this condition has been known to prove fatal.

Bacteria that cause food poisoning need warmth, food, moisture, and time to grow. The more you control these factors, the less likely they will succeed in compromising your patrons' health. The best temperature for most of these bacteria to grow is body temperature. i.e., 37°

Celsius. Since bacteria can grow anywhere between 5° and 63° Celsius, this range is called the danger zone. So, it is best to keep all cooked food at either below 5° or at above 63° Celsius.

The high-risk foods are proteinaceous ones such as meat, fish, poultry, eggs, dairy, etc., on which these microorganisms grow fastest. Bacteria grow best in the moistness of natural water, usually at a pH of 7 (i.e., neither too acidic nor alkaline). They grow by splitting into two. This multiplication takes around 10 to 12 minutes each time. As the process repeats, after an hour or so the quantity of bacteria present in the food becomes increasingly dangerous to eat.

To keep foods safely, store refrigerated foods at 1 to 4° Celsius, frozen foods at –18° Celsius and dry stores at 12° Celsius. While food must be cooked at 75° Celsius, it needs to be reheated at a higher temperature of around 82° Celsius.

Types of contamination:

- Physical: Foreign objects such as jewellery, glass, staples, nuts and bolts, or, soiled surfaces of equipment corners, clothes, etc., that can fall into the food.
- Biological: Bacteria or viruses passed on via sneezing/coughing, finger cuts, boils, pests, waste, etc.
- Chemical: Cleaning agents, pesticides, etc.

To prevent food contamination, it is necessary to get your team to strictly follow safety practices in your restaurant:

1. *Personal hygiene*

- Hands come most in contact with the food we prepare and must be washed thoroughly and frequently. Thoroughly meaning: With a strong soap from the tips of your nails till your exposed forearms for at least 20 seconds (I recall my food safety instructor suggesting singing 'Happy Birthday song' in one's mind or out loud if you must, to time the soaping). Frequently meaning: After using the toilet, gloves, the telephone, handling waste/cleaning chemicals, touching any other body parts, sneezing/coughing, and before handling any food/equipment, one must wash one's hands.

- Hair must only be combed in the toilet or changing room. Hair on the head and face must properly be covered with a hair cap and face mask to prevent the fall of hair/dandruff into the food.

- Skin infections/cuts/boils must be covered first with suitable bandages and then with waterproof disposable gloves.

- Jewellery must not be worn by food handlers as it may collect dirt more easily, drop into the food and even get caught in equipment/machinery.

- Uniforms: Clean clothing and non-slip covered shoes don't just help maintain safety but also help reinforce the image of cleanliness.

- Tasting Spoon: To prevent contamination while tasting, use a separate tasting spoon rather than the serving spoon that stays in the dish.

2. Clean and sanitize your space

While cleaning removes the visible physical dirt from a surface, sanitizing removes the invisible microorganisms from service-ware and equipment.

The correct method for cleaning and sanitizing dishes varies in each organization. Broadly, after scraping off the food remains from the dish, a pre-wash in plain tap water (warm or regular) is done. Dishes are then washed in warm water with a detergent using a cloth or brush. The soap is then rinsed off using warm clean water with a cloth or left to air dry. Of course, a dish washing machine helps reduce the time and labour involved.

3. Pest control

Pests such as cockroaches and flies carry diseases, while rats may also cause havoc by eating through cables, foods. etc. It is important to understand the habits and preferences of each pest with the help of your pest control agency to be able to defend your restaurant. Staying alert before matters escalate to an unmanageable level is the best practice. It is important to seal off possible pest entrances and sanitize all surfaces regularly.

4. Miscellaneous practices

- Keep food covered.
- Use separate utensils and chopping boards for raw and cooked food.
- Label raw food containers with their purchase date and follow the First In First Out practice.
- Reject cans that are swollen, dented, or rusted. (Once

you open a can, either use the contents immediately or then store them in another container inside the refrigerator).

- Label cooked food containers with their cooking date, time, and best consumed before labels, and follow the First Expired First Out practice.
- Ensure all vehicles and storage containers are clean.
- Store food on racks that are at least six inches off the ground.
- Discard unused reheated food within four hours of being removed from temperature controlled storage.
- Separate the usage of potable water for cleaning and cooking from the other water required for cleaning.

Should one of your guests or a group of them approach you claiming that they have suffered food poisoning due to food prepared at your restaurant, here are a few points to remember:

- If the matter has reached the food safety authorities, they will most likely be compelled to conduct an investigation. Rather than interfere in their enquiry, it is best to provide them with facts through the records you have maintained. If you have realized that it is indeed due to a lapse on your part, it is best to admit to your mistake and apologize publicly rather than letting the media take you to the cleaners.
- If the media has got a hold of this information before the investigation is complete, let your statement be that you would like the facts to present themselves

for everyone to see rather than comment further at this stage.

- Should it be proved that your food is responsible for their illness, you will need to compensate them.

Should you or a staff member be affected by food poisoning whether it is through your own restaurant or not, remember:

- Try and stop the vomiting (and diarrhoea, if any).
- Replenish fluids which are rapidly being lost.
- If it is a severe case, consult a doctor immediately.

The four core food safety processes that one needs to follow are:

1. **Clean:** Your own hands, your equipment, utensils, and your entire workspace frequently; check fruits and vegetables for any damage before rinsing under running tap water; use disposable paper towels rather than cloth towels to wipe your hands and food-contact surfaces.

2. **Separate:** Cooked and raw food as well as vegetarian and non-vegetarian foods to avoid cross-contamination via storage containers, cooking utensils, chopping boards, plates, etc.

3. **Cook:** Use a thermometer to check that foods are being defrosted, cooked, reheated, and served at their ideal temperatures with an eye on the time for which they are being kept.

4. **Chill:** Use a thermometer to check that foods are being stored before and after cooking at their ideal

temperatures, and only for a safe duration.

Overall, to be a food safety compliant enterprise you must:

- Conduct regular staff medical examinations and maintain records.
- Conduct frequent pest control initiatives and maintain their records.
- Take food temperatures daily (of food prepared, stored, and served) and maintain their records.
- Since food traceability is becoming increasingly important these days, maintaining the purchase records of food is also important. Restaurateurs are responsible for the condition of the raw materials that are stored on their premises, even if they have not yet been used, since they are a potential hazard if adulterated or spoilt.
- Use a maintenance tracking checklist to monitor all equipment and the upkeep of the entire facility at large and maintain their records.
- Conduct lab tests of water, food, and beverages as well as swab tests (hand- and food-contact surfaces).

These self-corrective measures keep you on the right side of the authorities and also of your guests should your food safety practices ever come into question. They provide evidence that your efforts are not just empty talk but diligent and genuine habits that are part of your work culture.

Supply Chain Traceability

Any restaurateur worth their salt wants to serve their guests food that is safe, tasty, cost effective, and convenient. He understands that among the many things they must do to achieve this, attention to the supply chain is critical. Further, their consumers may also want to know all sorts of things about the ingredients: where they are from, how fresh they are, how they were transported, etc., and why not? Anyone committed to good health and fair practices, whether a manufacturer or a consumer, is entitled to know.

Today, people expect a brief résumé of their ingredients and finished goods. Tomorrow, they will demand an entire dossier of traceable details on every aspect of the supply chain.

So, let's take the example of a simple ingredient such as an onion at the kitchen of a caterer. Now, imagine that we have to map this entire journey and share the details.

What better way to know your onions than to ask them. So, visualize an onion telling us about its journey...

From farm to plate

Farm

I was sown in August 2022 in Nashik, Maharashtra, harvested in Jan 2023, and sold in a jute sack at the Lasalgaon wholesale market at ₹9 per kilo. The excellent quality black loam soil with organic manure I was grown in, led to me to be a good-sized 50mm, A-grade Nashik Red Onion in the market that season.

Wholesale market

A local trader bought and stored me at ambient temperature around 30° C and a relative humidity (RH) of 65%. Since my neck had been dried for 10 days, I lost about 10% of my weight but stayed well without rotting or sprouting and you could hear the nice dry rustle in the 40kg sack each time we were periodically turned to prevent us from getting spoiled. In around three weeks, the trader sold me for ₹18 per kilo at the local mandi (market).

Restaurant

A restaurant brand called Swaad bought me for ₹36 per kilo via a retailer to whom we were sold by the trader. We were stored for a few days at the restaurant, after which we were peeled and chopped or sliced for cooking.

Plate: End consumer feedback

While the chefs were happy with us mostly, some of us that were unusable, were returned to be exchanged for an equivalent weight of usable onions.

Details mentioned in the above 'onion conversation' are meant only for representational purposes and not to be taken literally. In the food business, we must know not just our onions, but every single ingredient, whether raw or prepared, can be tracked at every step of our supply chain, i.e., from farm to plate. Honestly sharing this information with our stakeholders helps build trust in the brand and, thus, loyalty towards it.

Traceability of the Food Supply Chain

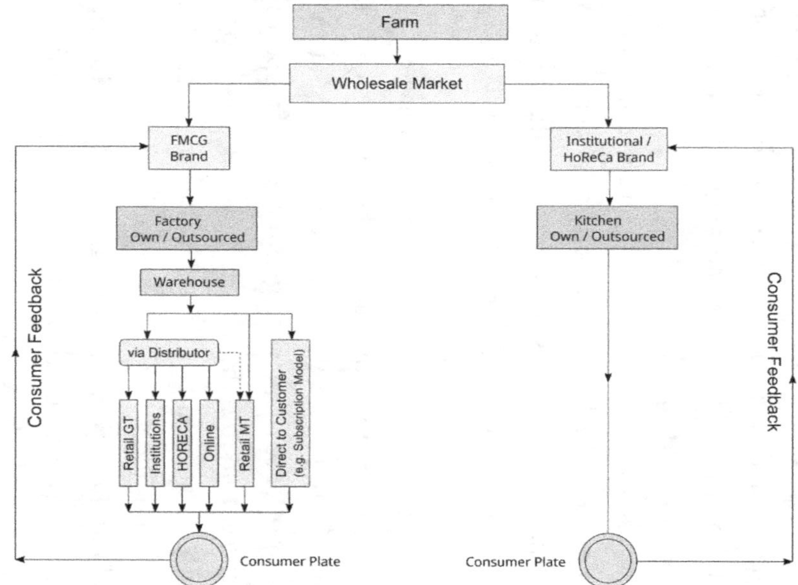

Glossary

FMCG: Fast Moving Consumer Goods
HoReCa: Hotels, Restaurants, Catering Companies
Institutions: HoReCa, Offices, Factories, Schools, Hospitals...
Retail MT: Modern Trade refers to organized retail including supermarkets, hypermarkets, convenience stores...
Retail GT: General Trade refers to traditional small scale kirana stores or grocery shops for small scale purchases.

Bridging Execution Gaps Caused by Perception Challenges

In business, as in life, things rarely go according to plan. We plan one thing, and something else 'happens'. Invariably, gaps exist between planning and execution. There are many factors which influence the smooth execution of a plan. One of these factors is the alignment between our perception and that of others.

There are some challenges clearly within our control and then some over which we have little or no control. While it is true that whatever has to go wrong will, we must still approach the execution of a plan by identifying which factors we can control and to what degree.

I was once conducting telephonic interviews for a standalone restaurant. For a few of the positions, my target candidates were people who were then serving at five-star hotels. Our offer to them was a greater level of responsibility and decision-making than they presently had, or, were likely to have at even two levels higher than their current positions. Initially, we were of the opinion that presenting potential candidates with this logic coupled with a salary raise would have them salivating at the opportunity.

Logical enough? Sure! Easy enough? Absolutely not!

It turned out that most candidates were hesitant even to further discussions beyond their first point of contact with our company, the HR department. Those that were 'open' were looking to be compensated at two or three times their present income. This was obviously difficult to absorb by even a well-budgeted restaurant chain. On delving further, I discovered that it was the perceptions of these candidates that led them to believe that a transition from a five-star hotel to a standalone restaurant would be a step down in their career. Their hesitation and unrealistic salary expectation stemmed from this perception of a 'downgrade'.

This is just one example of the many perception-based workplace challenges that we experience every day. In this case, our plan to present logic alone was limited in its ability to draw in talent.

So, we experienced difficulty in executing our hiring initiative. We were basically dealing with candidates whose perceptions far outweighed reality. Our first response had only focused on their role and salary. Only when we understood this, did we realize that we needed to work on managing our candidate perceptions as well.

Subsequently, we chose to augment the content of our presentation with something that we discovered was both relevant as well as important to the candidates. No spiel or false promises, just a greater focus on the brand aspects—the lens through which they perceived us—that we had neglected until then. What they wanted to know more about was the company and brand background, its existing brand presence internationally, and future intent. This information reassured them about what they were getting into and with whom. It armed them with more holistic information that was necessary for them to make a decision to join or consider joining us.

Once we did this, we met with success. Ironically, every person hired eventually was one who appreciated the logic, i.e., they recognized the long-term benefits of experiencing a greater level of responsibility and decision-making earlier in their career. So, the logic did work! But only when it was dovetailed with a deeper brand-related presentation, which, in this case, was pivotal to the successful execution of our hiring plan.

As individuals, all of us have beliefs which may not be well-founded. This often causes a gap between planning and execution. Such gaps may occur both in our own businesses as well as those of others. In the restaurant industry, all people groups–entrepreneurs, employees, vendors, and customers–are constantly interacting with one another. All of them are guilty of allowing their perceptions to control their decisions. We must be aware of this so we can understand where other people are coming from and wherever possible, do something about it.

Let's take a look at some perception-based scenarios which cause gaps between planning and execution.

Scenario 1:

A particular customer has always had a great experience at your restaurant. They now expect the same level of experience at the very least, every single visit. Next, out of conviction, they introduce their guests to your brand while highly recommending it.

Out of human error, more than one mishap occurs and they are not just severely disappointed but also embarrassed. The reason is that he attached his personal reputation to this lapse in experience.

We all know that human error is inevitable, regardless

of how well the brand standards are documented within a particular organization. Having documented Standard Operating Procedures are simply of no consequence if they are not well implemented.

It is, thus, far more important to first explain the rationale of these procedures to one's team in relation to every 'moment of truth' from the guest's perspective. Next, their regular practice must be encouraged. This is essentially the crux of actually 'delivering' a brand experience. Unless your team perceives the merit in this, they will neither be willing nor be able to execute your SOPs well. Only once this happens, can the guest perception of your experience be achieved.

Even then, an expectation of zero error is unreal, but at least the process would have begun.

Going forward, listening to your guest, directly and through your frontline employees gives you clues on how to further evolve your brand promise and be better aligned to the needs of your guests.

Scenario 2:

Many entrepreneurs complain about the difficulty in sourcing good people. They highlight how most candidates lie about their accomplishments, capabilities, salaries, intentions, etc. How they create false positive perceptions about their candidature and then fail to deliver. Yet these very entrepreneurs lie unabashedly to attract a 'good' candidate. They create false positive perceptions about their company's accomplishments, capabilities, turnover, future plans, etc., and then complain when things don't go as planned with the employee.

The reality is, that it is normal for most people (employers and potential employees) to present themselves to one another by putting their best foot forward. In fact, someone once said that an interview (in an extreme situation) is a discussion between two liars, both trying to convince one another by stretching the truth.

The way to find a median path will be for both sides to give each other an allowance of space for this. Deliverables always work best both ways in any relationship. An entrepreneur believing that making timely payments is their only deliverable will be just as mistaken as an employee who believes that showing up on time is their only deliverable.

While on the subject of hiring, a typical part of the process is that of a reference check. Such a check must be conducted by the right person asking the right questions. If this doesn't happen, it is likely to lead to a skewed decision on your shortlisted candidate. More importantly, how you deal with these reference check findings is crucial.

Let us consider a situation where an ex-employer is extremely biased towards his ex-employee. By 'extremely' I mean a statement (either positive or negative) about the candidate that influences your 'perception' enough to conclude your decision for or against the candidate. Human bias in such decisions is inevitable, particularly in India. We automatically become positively or negatively predisposed towards a candidate when we accept another's biases about him. We compliment ourselves on our 'findings' and justify our decisions accordingly. If a candidate draws praise from an ex-employer, we compliment ourselves on our own 'good judgement'. If a candidate draws criticism from an ex-employer, we also compliment ourselves on our own 'good judgement'.

Sadly, our newly-formed perception may take its toll only later in our relationship with the candidate. If the reference has positively and disproportionately praised the candidate and you hire him, you will eventually pay for not doing your homework when you discover that he is unable to deliver. If the reference has negatively and disproportionately criticized the candidate and you don't hire him, you will eventually pay for not doing your homework because you know deep within that you might have lost out on a really good employee.

Rather than letting someone else's opinion cloud your judgement, establish the facts. Whether you know the ex-employer or not, remind yourself that like you and the candidate, the ex-employer, too, is a human being subject to biases. Check for yourself rather than sabotage your own organization by creating a gap between the planning and execution of your hiring initiative.

Scenario 3:

An economy Udupi restaurant's expectation of a guest is to finish eating in let's say 20 minutes and leave. Guests accept this and so when a waiter places the check before them while they are still consuming their meal, it is considered alright. Pulling this off in other types of establishments has not been easy for the brands concerned.

When Cafe Coffee Day (CCD), for instance, started

offering the check alongside as well, guests initially found it hard to accept. But subtle repetitive communication to guests by their service staff slowly made it acceptable to them.

Coffee shops in India had for long been facing the consequences of customers just hanging around for hours without buying 'enough'. Over the course of time, guests discovered that CCD was, in fact, respectfully bringing to their attention that a certain period of time had lapsed since their first order. They also realized that the establishment was paying for this time and that subsequent orders from guests at regular intervals would help them rationalize their costs.

Some patrons though, still consider this practice unacceptable. Most, however, realize that it is only fair for an establishment to co-relate its high costs arising out of real estate etc., per hour with their guest's consumption/billing per hour. This is a wonderful example of not just a good plan to address this challenge but more importantly a well-executed one. Considering it involved changing consumer mindset—one of the toughest things to achieve in the business—it is a great accomplishment.

All these scenarios highlighted how people's perceptions play a role in their decision-making. We saw how these decisions, in turn, sometimes led to gaps between an organization's planning and execution, and also how some of these gaps can be filled.

A customer's decision on which brand to buy from, an employee's decision on which organization to pursue for work, an entrepreneur's decision on which vendor to appoint, are just few examples of the multitude of the perception-based decisions that happen every moment in the hospitality ecosystem.

Understanding and adapting ourselves to the needs and wants of various types of people in the marketplace is the first step. Once we do this, we inevitably align our thoughts, words, and actions more effectively with theirs. This is what proficiently bridges the gap between planning and execution!

The Value of Dissent

I was once a part of the senior leadership team at a large and old institutional catering firm, which had a great level of maturity in its decision-making. Its leaders, though extremely experienced, had their business ideas formally vetted by the rest of the leadership think tank through structured sessions while still retaining the final responsibility and accountability for each decision within their own business vertical.

The result was magically productive for both the individual leaders as well as the organization, even when the 'other side' won. The individuals went away exposed to alternate thinking that could be more productive in their respective businesses. Thus, each individual leader grew as a decision maker.

Another organization, a very young one I dealt with was unfortunately still to learn the value of dissent. The entrepreneur's philosophy was, "If you want to do it your way, you'd best do it in your own business, not here". In other words, "I do the thinking around here, you are only here to execute". Every staff member who stayed on with the organization simply played along, worked mechanically, and never dared to tell him the truth. Only, what he wanted to hear.

Imagine you are making multiple decisions that you intend to live with, in your business. The buck certainly stops with you. But are you really the most 'intelligent' person in your business for every single decision? Isn't it better to actively seek the wisdom of others in your team on some decisions at least? Are you able to listen with an open mind to alternate views not aligned with your own? Can you afford to ignore the potential power of collective thinking?

Professionalizing a Family-Run Restaurant

"We are a family-run business. We have a good team that we would like to improve through training and also bring some professionals on-board. It's so tough to find good people these days."

"We would like better systems and processes so we can expand and also work well even in our absence, as we can take holidays without the worry of wondering what's going on when we aren't around."

"We have been doing well since three generations. However, each of us have a different vision and approach towards our business. What is the right way forward?"

World over, restaurants run by families echo these thoughts.

It's certainly true that finding and retaining good talent these days is difficult, even in a professionally-run organization with a slick image that pays well. But before we get to that, there is something more crucial to start with.

Get your act together internally first

1. If within your co-founders, you don't each have a clear set of responsibilities and speak with one voice, fix that first. Without further delay go ahead and allocate responsibilities and agree on the fundamental direction of the business to avoid work overlaps and conflicts.
2. Be clear about who is going to take decisions in which area of the business and stick to that plan.
3. Be in agreement amongst yourselves about whether your business really needs someone from the outside. If so, decide what you expect that person to focus on initially, what you expect them to achieve and in what timeframe, and how you all will truly 'allow' them inside your business and give them the kind of support that will set them up for success.

This 'outsider' may be a consultant or an executive that you need to help bring about the change you envision, basically a 'Change Agent'.

Business goals in which you may need a Change Agent

- To improve efficiencies within your business or optimize/stabilize it.
- To re-engineer or sell your businesses.

- To grow it.
- To groom your next generation into the business and have them well supported (even if they have just graduated from a reputed business school).
- To retire or simply wean yourself away from your business.

In such circumstances, a Change Agent could help you not just achieve your goal, but could also free up your time to concentrate on things you really need to do or would like to do.

The right Change Agent must

- Respect what your team or family you have created so far.
- Understand why you need them and what is expected of them.
- Be happy with the task at hand and have an entrepreneurial comfort with ambiguity.
- Have enough industry knowledge to assess what will be required to achieve your goals reasonably soon after they have been adequately immersed into your brand.
- Have the resilience to adapt to a work environment like yours where their prior knowledge of how things get done might be constantly challenged.
- Communicate objectively all around and express their concerns consistently to remain true to your organizational objectives despite the challenges of people dynamics.

- Have a temperament that makes you and your family comfortable enough so that if change means that "you" need to change, you will listen with an open mind and work on making that change yourself.

Now, let's say that you agree that this is indeed the kind of person you need to hire, but feel that finding such a person is a tall order. You are right, it certainly isn't easy. You may not get someone with all these qualities in the exact manner that you envision. You must first be clear about which of these ideals are necessary and which are desirable in your candidate.

Next, you must consider the concept of an interim hire versus a permanent one. Across the world, the tenure of an interim executive ranges anywhere from 90 days to 3 years—not very different from a permanent CXO one these days and at times better for your business.

Lastly, being well connected, as we are with social networks today, offers the opportunity to reach out far and wide to multiple and diverse groups. These groups are likely to know a person who could fit the profile you are looking for.

Your approach towards a Change Agent

Once you have the person on-board, do your best not just to keep him but to make each interaction with him a good one, and that starts with you making that effort.

The best place to start, as with any relationship, is trust, and that begins with clarity.

- Convey to the Change Agent the scope of responsibility and decision-making of each co-director whom they will report into.
- Share your concerns about problematic people and pain points of the business.
- Express what you are unsure about.
- Be open to the fact that they may see things completely differently from the current perspective of anyone in your organization.
- Let go of past preconceived notions or baggage that your team and you may be carrying without realizing or admitting it, even to yourselves. It is hard for us as human beings to be shown a mirror.
- Give them genuine permission to do what you have commissioned them for, and motivate others to do the same, in the interest of the greater good.

It is said that professionalising a family and friends' business is often brought about by working on its people and processes, and that is true. But one must remember that working with people and processes means working with mindsets.

An organization's mindset is made up of both individual and collective voices that rule decisions. Pay attention to which aspects of your organization's mindset might be blocking its development. Remember our beliefs and habits are usually a matter of our inheritance and experience. Changing them takes an extraordinary amount of commitment, time, and rigour.

Think of your own undesirable habits, both in your

professional and personal life, and recognize that even though you may like to change the habits which you know are harming you, practically doing so is easier said than done. Also, be aware of the presence of hidden agendas and biases, and the fact that taking corrective action is by no means easy.

So, take the time to recognize what your Change Agent is up against and treat him accordingly. Remember that he is here to complete you and your team in terms of fulfilling your business goals. Individual accountability is important, but if it leads to finger pointing, then it subverts the ability to collaborate with him and defeats the very purpose of the association.

Should you see conflict between him and a devoted team member who has been with you forever, try and first establish the facts before you take sides. If you'd like 'objectivity' to rule supreme in your organization, it may be wisest to take the side of whichever suggestion best serves the interests of the business.

I am not implying that your Change Agent's suggestions will always be better than the decisions your existing team and you have taken or will take. Simply, that one should allow for this new team member to infuse fresh thought and deeply consider whether each of these thoughts will benefit your organization. If that fresh thought does improve things, put aside egos and embrace it. If not, decline that Change Agent's suggestion to encourage an enduring relationship and also to send a signal to your existing team about how you would like to do things from then on.

If you find that you both are not on the same page quite

often, then you may need to revisit your goals with the Agent and, if necessary, also revisit the continuance of their services.

Regardless of your specific goals, remember that your main objective is to professionalize your business by improving its existing practices and habits. In this context, Benjamin Franklin's words ring true: "Your net worth to the world is usually determined by what remains after your bad habits are subtracted from your good ones."

There are occasions when despite your efforts, either your Change Agent fails you, or, only completes a part of your mandate. In such situations, trusting someone again or starting over, becomes hard. Keep in mind that your true purpose of hiring this person is to nurture your family business by giving it whatever it needs so that it can in turn give you what you all need. You will be doing your business a great disservice if you allow circumstances or lack of patience to get in the way of being its true guardian.

Finally, to move from where you are at to where you need to be, be prepared to switch from management mode to leadership mode. As Steven Covey points out, "Management is efficiency in climbing the ladder of success; leadership determines whether the ladder is leaning against the right wall."

How to Grow Your Restaurant Business

Food and Beverage (F&B) operators who have successfully set-up their first restaurant, often find it hard to figure out how they should grow. Whether to choose the franchise route, go in for a joint venture, or simply grow organically, is often confusing.

Let's look at an informed approach to answer these questions decisively, but first things first:

Why do you want to grow?

Flattered by a prospective investor, a restaurateur with a successful outlet once began his expansion journey by giving up a controlling share of 51% to his new partner. They agreed it was realistic to roll out three new outlets in their first year, but within a few months found that they couldn't agree on the locations. The reason—the restaurateur was driven more by his love for the brand, while the investor simply had a cold, hard financial perspective. Regardless of who was right, the restaurateur found himself regretting the partnership. Essentially, he had not thought through the extent to which brand reach and financial return motivated him to grow in the first place. Furthermore, he hadn't discussed specifics of what was right for the business with his future partner before signing him up.

Asking yourself what is right for you and for your business is a good place to start.

Where are you now?

The owner of an eatery had created what appeared to be an interesting business model. The production process of the outlet mirrored that of McDonald's. A pancake, for instance, was made by placing a mould on the griddle with a prescribed volume of batter poured into it. This was followed by a predetermined cooking temperature and prescribed time on either side of the pancake, till it was done to perfection. Everything was great, except that the outlet was losing money. Its target audience found the product expensive in relation to better quality options and more economically available ones nearby.

On pointing this out to the owner, he responded that in order for the brand to be 'scalable', he saw wisdom in procuring high-quality raw materials, even if they were at a higher cost and meant absorbing losses temporarily. I maintained that since we would get no discount or cost benefit for scaling up, at least from this vendor, we should procure it from elsewhere or manufacture it ourselves. He disagreed and eventually was forced to shut down his business.

The point here is that all existing restaurants have flaws—planning their scale-up without:

a) Differentiating between the acceptable flaws and the potentially fatal ones and,
b) Acting on the flaws that matter, before actually growing the business can be disastrous.

Correct the key mistakes in your existing outlet before thinking about growth.

What attitudes might help during growth?

I once raced 100cc motorcycles for a company called Sports-Craft. This bunch of experts I raced with included automobile engineers and mechanics who understood their vehicles well. Their sole agenda was to move their vehicles from point A to point B in the shortest possible time with the risk and potential damage duly considered. This is very much like our own agenda of moving businesses from where they are currently at to where we would like them to be, as quickly as possible. In that sense, you are in fact racing with time.

An attitude of racing means:

- Stripping your vehicle of its lights, engine guard, and even fuel, to the bare minimum required. In our context, your vehicle is your business format like a QSR, Fine Dine, Kiosk, etc., with an in-house or an outsourced central kitchen, which must be kept lean.
- In an uphill climb (read your business growth challenge), keep less air pressure than prescribed in your front tyre and more than prescribed in your back tyre. This will help the front tyre grip the road and the back one bounce well enough to take the bends in the road. I liken this in the business context to staying well connected with consumer demand and being flexible to turn in the direction of consumer preferences.
- When confronted with an unavoidable small obstacle in your path, hit it head on with a firm grip on your handle bars. It is most likely that after a bit of a wobble, your vehicle will straighten up and stabilize. If not, take the fall and ride the skid as you would in your business.

To race, you require a vehicle, a track, and, of course, a driver.

If your business format represents the type of vehicle in the race, let's see what your driver and track symbolize.

Your drivers are inevitably the market demand and your own desire to serve your audiences and profit from them.

The track is the infrastructure, including government policy, licensing, real estate, manpower, etc. If you find these things challenging, rather than simply complain about them, see what you can do to help bring about improvements. Invest effort in supporting the transformation of these problems via trade bodies, federations, and associations that represent the sector. They can influence change in the long run, and therefore supporting them will help overcome these issues and give you a voice in the direction of change. This process, however, will be slow. Recognizing that and focussing on areas over which we have greater control in our business will serve us well.

Prepare yourself for growth with a racer's attitude and focus on what is important.

What aspects should you focus on?

Break the priority barrier

When I ask a restaurateur how they spend their time each day, I typically get a checklist of what looks like an operations manager's task sheet. I remind them that they would do better by focussing their efforts towards working on the business rather than in it. As an example, my own first business was Sun Catering, a meal service. Soon after it took flight, things got busy and I found myself unable to afford a professional manager to oversee the day-to-day operations and believed that I was the best person to represent my business, since I understood it best. I marketed it myself, cooked when I threw out a thieving chef, and prided myself at being a one-man army. However, when I fell ill, the business floundered, and I realized that I had failed to build a system that worked in my absence. I was the system and if something went wrong with me, it directly impacted the business. I should have realized that it was time to risk the second round of money (the first being my punting on the start-up itself) by spending on good people and manning the business in a way that it worked at least on maintenance mode without me. Establishing a system helps an entrepreneur stay free to do what they should do at this stage of their business... implement tweaks to resolve problems, chart the path for growth, and lead their team to success.

Gauge the resources you have and what you need

Ask yourself whether or not you have the time, money, and expertise pivotal for business growth and, if so, to what extent. Do you have other commitments? Is your present time away from the business spoken for? Is the time that you have enough to grow the business or will you need to bring in an outsider? In terms of expertise, are you equipped or do you need help? One approach of a self-taught entrepreneur is to leap off the mountain and build his wings as he progresses through his journey. Can the business afford this learning curve at this stage? Do you have the money for growth or do you need an investor? Will he only invest money or time and expertise as well? Even if you have the money, is it worth risking your own, or, is it better to share your risk with someone else who has skin in the game?

Introspection on these questions will help you decide whether or not you need an outsider in your business, and if so, in which areas. It will tell you whether you should retain or relinquish a controlling share in your business, whether the person you bring in should be an employee, consultant, or partner, how junior or senior the person should be, etc.

These are points to consider when deciding whether to grow organically, through the franchise route, or via a joint venture. Your needs guided by a mentor will help you arrive at this decision.

Think like an investor

As with any investment like stocks or real estate where you evaluate the risk-to-return ratio, a restaurateur must wear his investor hat to evaluate his investment in growth. Even if you conclude that you will not be bringing in an investor, remember that you are staking your reputation and that of your brand, which you have worked hard to build.

Critically evaluate your own business on the basic areas that an investor will look at:

- The market potential of your concept: How strong is your value proposition in terms of scale and frequency of demand?
- Your financials: On the premise that your first outlet has been profitable for a while, what is the likelihood that your brand will be profitable in other locations as well and to what extent?
- Your team competence: Do you and your team have the capability to take the brand to the next level?

- Your business model: Its scalability and plan for income, marketing, risk mitigation, and exit.
- Your brand differentiation: USP such as patented recipes, process, etc., that will allow you to keep going when standing up against competition.

Keep a balance between wearing your restaurateur hat and your investor hat. Don't get caught up in either one.

To summarize:

- Look within for motivators.
- Keep a racer's attitude.
- Be aware of your drivers, vehicles, and track.
- Correct your mistakes before planning a scale up.
- Choose your associates and decide how you will work with them.
- Plan well. Know that despite your planning, things can go wrong and they will.
- Beyond a point, stop planning and take the plunge into the race for growth.

Getting Your Restaurant Franchise-Ready

"I've been getting enquiries to franchise my restaurant. I'm keen, but not sure how to go about it." Nowadays, restaurateurs with one or two outlets, newly-launched or old, already successful or yet to break-even, often get approached for a franchise. It is indeed flattering! It tells the owner that their restaurant is worthy of cloning, investing in, and can earn a good return. However, jumping into it without planning the depth and breadth of a franchise association puts their hard-earned reputation at stake and dilutes the very essence of their growth plan.

So, here's how you can get your restaurant franchise-ready…

The Assessment

A restaurateur must first honestly look inside and out to assess the brand's clone-worthiness:

Inside:

Potential franchisees invest in a franchisor's business on the premise that it is profitable and has been so for a while. If that is not the case, it is just not fair to offer someone a franchise. In fact, it is a breach of trust—without a doubt the worst way to start a relationship.

Outside:

Validate the potential demand for the brand in other locations by pilot testing it; this is really important. Though not foolproof, it's a good way to gather indicative consumer responses.

Move forward only once this is done.

The Approach

The book McDonald's: Behind the Arches by John F. Love points out how prioritizing the franchisee's profitability over their own builds a strong foundation. This approach built not just their franchisees' trust, but led to the franchisees themselves becoming McDonald's best brand ambassadors. This is the core of the franchisor-franchisee relationship.

- Franchisors who are only interested in securing their royalties and other sources of income from their franchisees, inevitably fail.
- A written legal document must certainly stem from a gentleman's agreement, but it is the spirit of the agreement which forms the premise on which the franchise's success rests.

The Replication

A franchisor must first be aware of existing problems within their business (particularly if they are cultural or system-related). They must ideally resolve these problems before franchising, or else with each new outlet their problems will multiply.

They must create and share a business plan with their franchisee which covers:

- The format (kiosks, quick service restaurants, etc.).
- Space requirement.
- Menu alterations.
- Equipment list.
- General layout.
- Staff required.
- Financial projections (including franchise fees, and profit or loss in different sales scenarios).

Of course, the information you share before your franchisee signs up is only a part of what's enough for them to take an informed decision.

The Search

Franchisees who would like to invest in the business' success may be:

- Known people like the restaurant's customers, associates, or family, or
- Unknown ones contacted through an advertisement or a franchise agency's database.

Whichever way a franchisee is found, their integrity and attitude come first. Only then will their ability to invest time and money, and their prior experience in the industry be of value.

Agreement Terms

Legal counsel is necessary to create an agreement that protects the interests of both parties. An advocate with franchising experience is ideal. Overall the agreement should cover:

- Rights over the brand/trademark ownership.
- Rights over the intellectual property ownership and confidentiality.
- Indemnity of the franchisor by the franchisee.
- Non-compete clause.
- Legal, financial, and social obligations and deliverables of each party.
- Franchise fees and payment dates, both one-time and ongoing (other payments to the franchisor such as rent for special equipment, food rate per kilo, etc.).

- Operating practices and terms such as access to franchisee's cash register, personal involvement of franchisee, etc.
- Territory exclusivity.
- Change or transfer of shareholding.
- Terms of agreement—renewal and termination.

Inducting a franchisee into your brand

Training

A franchisor inducts a franchisee by training them on how to run the business commercially, technically, and as a hospitable host. This is usually done by getting the franchisee to spend some hands-on time at the franchisor's restaurant as well some specific discussions and training programs for the franchisee and their team.

Manuals

Written manuals to be shared usually touch upon the brand philosophies, organizational hierarchy, contact personnel for assistance, standard operating procedures (in terms of purchase, storage and the preparation of food and its service), human resource policies, and, generally, the quality and standards expected in every aspect of the business.

Management information

A dashboard of management information shared between the franchisor and franchisee helps both parties monitor the business performance continually and take decisions and corrective action.

Purchase

The franchisor must identify which existing vendors the franchisee will have to purchase from centrally, and which they may purchase by themselves locally. For example, a franchisor may insist that the franchisee buy a certain brand of equipment, but may be open to the franchisee sourcing, say vegetables, themselves.

Outlet design

Preparing an outlet design docket before a franchisee signs up his outlet, rather than after, saves a lot of time and money. Though each specific layout would eventually need to be custom-planned, putting down the design details and broad quantities of furniture, floor type, etc., must be done in advance.

Marketing

Simply taking 2% or more of a franchisee's sales for this, particularly if a franchisor has just one or two outlets, is meaningless. It is more prudent to compile a list of sales initiatives you propose for the franchisee's business and work out their costs. Sharing this plan with the franchisee and letting them know that they need to foot the entire amount to build sales at their own outlet is a more realistic and transparent method.

There are a host of consultants and agencies in the marketplace who can help you in each or many of these areas. You can choose which areas you can cover yourself and in which areas you will need help. Regardless, it is you who must drive the overall process and orientation of your franchising endeavour.

Section IV

Weathering Difficult Times

The pandemic was the biggest storm the restaurant industry faced globally. Many were forced to shut down. "The water got inside them."

The savings of many restaurants, even those that had survived for over a decade, weren't enough to tide them over for so many months without an income. It was really hard for restaurateurs to renegotiate their rents with their landlords, especially since some of them were dependent on this rental income for their own living. Not being able to pay their staff salaries was heartbreaking for restaurateurs, particularly facing those team members who had served with them for years. Many staff members threw in the towel, never to return. Some restaurateurs even took loans, but couldn't pay back. The expense of complying with COVID-19 equipment, practices of 50% occupancy only, limited hours of operation, etc., further took its toll. Some colleagues lost family members and some wonderful restaurateurs and their teammates themselves passed away. It was traumatic!

But the human capacity to absorb pain and bounce back is far greater than one might imagine and when the storm subsided, many restaurateurs (old and new) set sail once again with even greater journeys planned.

After the temporary consciousness of hygiene during the pandemic, customers went back to their favourite roadside stalls... some of which were cleaner than before. The rise of home deliveries by restaurants during COVID-19 continued (partly because homes served as offices then and some continue to do so), even as the desire to dine out at restaurants began booming again.

Pre-pandemic problems like attracting and retaining staff, not being allowed to offset taxes that restaurants pay, heavy government regulations, aggregators eating up margins etc., however, still continue.

Let us take a look at the many challenges we are likely to be faced within the restaurant business, and how we can better prepare ourselves to deal with them. But before that let me start with a personal example.

I was 19, studying at the Institute of Hotel Management (IHM), Mumbai, riding home on my motorcycle, when suddenly a man pushing a two-wheeler hand cart appeared out of nowhere, just a few feet in front of me and on seeing me, abandoned his cart and ran. To my right was a metal road divider covered with signage that had blocked my visibility and his. To my left were moving vehicles, and in front of me the empty cart. Pressing the brakes hard and instantly at that distance, meant a certain crash, so attempting a jump on what was now an unstable ramp was my only option. No helmets back then, since reports at the time, showed they caused more head injury through splintering in a crash, than save. Three days later, on regaining consciousness, I learnt that I had had a concussion, plus stitches on my lip and eyelid. With much care from my kind family and the sympathetic doctors at Nair hospital, I recovered.

I decided that if I'm ever faced with such an obstacle again, I must successfully jump it. I enrolled myself in Sports-Craft, a motor sports club with committed leaders and terrific riders, including automobile engineers and mechanics. Its supportive ecosystem offered me an understanding of vehicle control, speed and safety, and good quality helmets, of course.

Participating in the 100cc Indian bike category uphill climb, with such formidable opponents, I knew I would never be in the top race league, but my endeavour was important enough for me then to take the risks that went with it.

When I finally made my jump on a six-feet mud ramp (standing high on my bike, with my top wheel around 20-feet off the ground), it was scary, especially to land on my back-wheel alone, without falling. But that's what it took to make me feel that I had achieved my objective.

In the many obstacles that life presents, I have found it useful to identify which ones require a head-on approach like this and which ones... an alternate route.

An entrepreneur faces a significant number of obstacles day after day. How you learn from today's mistakes to prepare for a better tomorrow, is the key.

Self-Defence during a Recession

If there's one thing we have learnt from the pandemic, it is to be better prepared. I recommend focussing on three things to start with:

Operational efficiency

Many entrepreneurs and managers are doing 'step-down' jobs these days—essentially what their subordinates are supposed to do. Partly because they are stressed about the possibility of losing their business or their jobs and partly because they may have already let a few of their team members go and are short-staffed. While ordinarily this is considered to be poor management, the fact remains that extraordinary times call for extraordinary actions.

Going back to basics, it is the important and urgent tasks like meeting customer demands that come first (if you don't have a customer, you don't have a business), followed by meeting shareholder demands (if this is not being met, the intent of the promoters will dissolve and the business will no longer exist).

All initiatives of a business inevitably stem from these larger goals, not just normally, but particularly in present conditions.

Cost effectiveness

In a situation where demand and sales are random and uncertain, slashing costs ruthlessly is the greatest temptation. However, beyond a point a business cannot reduce its costs without compromising on the delivery of its promise. So, what do we do?

Considering each cost component of our business, one at a time and seeing which of them can be rationalized and how, would be the best way forward.

Let's look at some…

A franchised waffle outlet moved shop from a high-end building to a nearby basic one, and slashed its rent by 40% with no drop in sales, as the same customers were willing to walk 200 meters more for them.

An Italian casual dining restaurant, gave its general manager and executive chef a 5% incentive of its profit in addition to their salaries on the agreement that the owners would be less present so that they could grow more outlets and that their salaries would not be increased until the recession was completely over.

Likewise, other costs must be duly and fairly assessed for potential in reductions.

Customer centricity

Value is something that even the wealthiest look for in an offer. Of course, value means different things to different people and depends on the nature of the proposition as well. In a mid-level proposition, free toys included with kids' meals may be considered value, whereas in a high-end place, it could be personalized chopsticks with the names of loyal patrons engraved for use when they visit. At the most basic level, customers might simply want the best food at the lowest price.

Customers always measure your offer in terms of quantity and quality in relation to the price they pay. They quickly base their expectations according to the type of format (kiosk, sit-down, etc.) and the level (casual dining, fine dining, etc.), and compare it with other similar propositions in the market place. Propositions that keep evolving their offer to meet customer needs and wants survive, while those that exceed customer expectations thrive.

Brands that engage their guests by providing an all-round sensory experience, make memories for them that result in a greater emotional connect. This is what generates loyalty towards the brand.

Delivery of guest satisfaction these days would involve being more conscious of guest feedback in terms of needs and wants and adapting your proposition accordingly. So, for instance, bundling products to offer value combo meals at a mid-level brand is likely to be well received.

A focus on these areas is most likely to reward the overall development or evolution of the business through this phase of the economy.

Correcting guest experiences gone wrong

Businesses with even the most customer-oriented focus may have guest experiences that go wrong. Correcting such experiences requires both awareness and a conscious effort—though on occasion, unfortunately, correction may not be possible.

Here are a few of many I have had:

I looked at the elderly guest in shock and then at the cake splattered on the floor that he had just thrown in my direction. "You call this fresh cream?" he screamed angrily. I knelt on the floor and dug into the cake with my finger. "You're right, sir. This isn't fresh at all. In fact, besides being sour, the cream has also absorbed the smell of the dishes in your fridge. I'm sorry," I said, "When did you buy this?"

He looked at me sort of surprised that I actually tasted it and then he cooled down a bit.

"Day before yesterday, in the evening—for my wedding anniversary which was yesterday. When we cut the cake in front of our guests and tasted the first bite, my wife and I knew we couldn't serve it to our guests," he said.

A quick look at the label on the cardboard base confirmed when he had bought it. "This is entirely our fault, sir. We should have communicated to you that our fresh cream cakes don't last that long and should be consumed within a few hours. We take complete responsibility."

He accepted a refund and trudged away sadly.

I discussed this communication gap with everyone in my team and in a few days we had a solution. He was surprised when I called him a week later to ask if I may visit him just for five minutes.

When I handed him a cake box with a label on top saying 'Best Consumed Within Six Hours', and the message piped on the cake simply saying 'Sorry, We Messed Up', he nodded in acknowledgement. In those days, such labels were not much in use as they are now. We, at the Taj, were probably among the earliest, if not the first to start it.

"You listened and acted. Well done!"

"It wasn't just me, sir. Everyone on the team worked together to come up with this. We would like you to know that your feedback is truly valuable to us. Please do give us another chance."

To regain the lost trust, you can't just convey this to the customer through verbal apology, you must show him through your actions.

* * *

I was once called to a table at a restaurant I was working at by an actor who told me the fish served to her was raw in the centre. I apologized and took it away to the chef who decided to make good the problem by cooking it himself.

After a short while, it was re-served to the guest. I was again called to the table. This time along with the chef. "It's still raw," she said.

We stood stunned and soon went red-eared in embarrassment. After a few awkward moments of silence, I summoned the courage to speak. "I am truly sorry, ma'am," I said. "May I please offer you something else instead?"

"No," she said, "I am not hungry anymore." I felt like sinking through the floor and could see the chef squirming as well.

The lady watched us both, quite red-eyed by now and then with unforgettable grace, she said, "Don't worry. I'm OK. Bad days happen!"

We bowed out, went to the back of the restaurant, and wept. In one stroke, she had taught us about forgiveness and about how response matters more than situation one is in. Every server on our team that day learned that lesson.

Ever since, whenever she visits any restaurant that any one of us has moved to, we serve her with a different kind of respect, one reserved for nobility. This yoga-loving celebrity, was Indian film actor Shilpa Shetty.

* * *

The dimly-lit ground floor restaurant of the hotel I was once working in had been beautifully renovated and sported large French-window style glass sheets for the sunlight to pop in and add cheer.

Things looked terrific till one busy day I heard the violent crashing sound of glass shattering. I whirled to see the playful little boy who had run into it, standing in a pool of splintered glass.

He looked at me for a moment and then began to cry. I ran towards him, as did a guest nearby to see a trickle of blood run down his nose and also from his elbow.

His mother, the only adult at the table who was dining with her two kids, screamed at her other child and then, quite understandably, went berserk.

I placed my handkerchief on his bleeding nose, asked one elderly waiter to hold it, and sent another to fetch the hotel driver and car. "We need to take him to the hospital now, ma'am," I said loudly to pull her out of her daze. On our way to the hospital, I discovered that they were from out of town.

She gratefully acknowledged our assistance while I waited for the boy's nose to be stitched up. My mind, however, was pondering on the shattering of the glass. How did this happen? There was a clearly visible three-inch sticker strip running across the whole length of the window.

When I returned to the spot, I realized the height of the sticker was easily visible to an adult, but not to a child.

Whilst ordering a new glass I suggested that the complete bottom half be fully covered with a glazed sticker, and more importantly, that the glass be shatter-proof, despite the high cost.

The directors initially wondered if I was overreacting as they thought it was a freak incident and that it wouldn't happen again. However, when I stood my ground on the premise of safety, everyone agreed.

When a problem doesn't seem like a problem from one perspective, resolving it conclusively requires a shift in perspective.

* * *

While studying Hotel Management as a teenager at IHM, Mumbai, we were encouraged to attend to and serve real guests at 'waitings'. Typically, after college, we would be assigned to a specific event for the evening that was being catered to by a reputed hotel or caterer and be required to support their full-time wait staff. Apart from the experience, what also lured us was the cash allowance for the evening and a good meal, sometimes even a drink.

On one such occasion, I was partnering with the senior steward of a five-star hotel at a wedding at the Hinduja Bungalow at Juhu beach. He gave me a tray which looked like the dishes on it were already on the verge of toppling over and pointed, "Go out there to the pier on the beach and serve it to that table… the one that's currently occupied. Remember to wish them by their names."

Balancing a heavy tray laden with food can be extremely tricky, especially with uneven carpets and wires running across the ground. After I had walked most of the way, I realized that I hadn't asked him their names. As I approached the table, however, I saw a very familiar face, one that I'd seen on the big screen so many times that he didn't need an introduction. He was with his wife and kids. I clutched on to my tray, trudged onward, and wished them all as I reached.

As I looked at the table, I realized it was filled with accessories—a vase, an ashtray, and what not. With no sideboard nearby to place my tray on and such a heavy tray that I couldn't hold it one hand, I wondered how I'd make space for the dishes I was carrying.

He saw that and smiled. Then, most graciously and casually, he rearranged things on the table to make place. I immediately felt a sense of relief and respect for him.

I learnt then that while it takes a certain distinction to be a good host, it takes even more to be a good guest. My extraordinary guest was Amitabh Bachchan!

***

Attracting and Retaining Talent during a Recession

Let's look at the approaches and outcomes of two neighbouring restaurateurs A and B.

Mr. A protected his restaurant by slashing labour costs heavily. He kept only a few necessary people (on reduced salaries) that were required to manage the operation, and fired the rest. He believed that in a market where so many restaurant workers were losing their jobs, the few that he kept would never dare to leave since there were no jobs available.

Mr. B knew he had to cut costs as well. He took his team into his confidence and told them that he needed to reduce the total salaries by 50% and there were two ways he could do it. Either fire half the staff or keep everyone at half salary. He left the choice with his team. When the staff asked for them all to be retained at half pay, he offered them several on-the-spot incentives for whichever of them came up with cost-saving initiatives that didn't compromise the long-term credibility of the brand.

As expected, Mr. A found the staff morale of his remaining team members dropping. They knew they could also be axed at any time. Productivity began suffering and their customers bore the brunt of it. The little business that they were left with began shifting to their competitor Mr. B, whose genuinely hospitable staff made their guests feel truly welcome.

Additionally, two of Mr. A's laid-off star employees, the Purchase Supervisor and Marketing Manager, moved on to work for Mr. B. They were encouraged by the work ethos and team spirit there. Not only did the hiring of these two new employees pay immediate dividends, but it also became clear that their work culture at Mr. B's supported the likelihood of their long-term retention.

On exiting the recession, Mr. A's restaurant attracted only opportunistic employees whose intentions had a proportionate impact on its customers. On the other hand, restaurateur B attracted talent with far more honourable intentions, and that, too, had a proportionate impact on its customers.

While this example, of course, is purely hypothetical, the approaches and outcomes mentioned here are very much real and, in fact, closely resemble those of many companies nowadays.

The circumstance of each business is always unique and must be addressed accordingly. What remains constant is the fact that their choices today will have a certain impact on their outcomes tomorrow and many days thereafter.

Speaking about customers, as you may know, some are bad news. Here's a bit about dealing with such people.

Throwing Out Customers Who Aren't 'God'

When one of the most customer-centric managers I know, told me that one of our fairly regular guests at the restaurant had turned rogue, and that our team, who knew her well, just didn't know how to deal with her anymore, it certainly got my attention.

I learnt that on each of her last half dozen visits, she had claimed that we had been repeatedly disappointing her. Still, she continued to patronize us on the pretext of 'giving us more chances' while bullying our staff and demanding a discount on every single visit. This time, she had completely lost it and stormed out dramatically without paying her bill at all.

I watched the CCTV footage which showed her with an accompanying guest who was visibly embarrassed at her not paying the bill. Her guest, who clearly disagreed with her stance, offered to pay for the meal herself, but our friend stopped her from doing so. I played back the footage only to see our staff members squirming at the entitled, rude and unfair manner in which she behaved, while her guest looked on helplessly. The manager and I knew we had to bring this to its logical conclusion. We agreed that the next time she visited, we'd ask her to pay her last bill, failing which she'd no longer be welcome at our restaurant.

It wasn't long before she visited again, this time with another friend. To avoid embarrassing her in front of her guest, the manager took her aside and with all the courtesy extended to our regulars, requested her to clear her dues before we seated and served her. She declined, and so he proceeded to very politely and definitively tell her that since at each visit in the recent past we'd been unable to deliver on her expectations, it would be best that she took her business elsewhere and that we would not be in a position to serve her anymore.

Stunned for a moment, she soon gathered herself and stormed out once again, this time for good. Our full-house of guests and their happy banter stood testimony to the fact that we were delivering on our brand promise on most occasions.

While I support the sentiment that our customer is God, a giver of life so to speak, of the business, unreasonable guests like this are bad for business and must be expelled.

Crossing the line

Anyone in customer experience knows that a customer's anger stems either from a mistake made by the business that served him or from some emotional baggage that they themselves may have carried into the premises from the outside. Either way, it is only human for a customer who is upset to let off some steam on our team, or, even on other guests at times. It is also normal, once in a while, to be unreasonably demanding or badly behaved. On occasion, it also happens that a customer insults, abuses, or threatens us.

Rudeness is contagious and on such occasions it is our natural instinct to respond with equal disrespect. As service industry professionals however, we endeavour to rise above this.

If a guest's anger has originated due to our fault, we obviously try and make amends so as not to lose our customer. If instead, it isn't our mistake, we still want to maintain peace in the situation.

Regardless, we must respond maturely, managing human anger with compassion. Our efforts towards empathy and an apology to an enraged guest are most critical.

If despite such efforts, our customer continues to misbehave by insulting, abusing, or threatening us, we must appeal to them one final time possibly using words like, "Look, I'm very sorry that you had to go through this. I understand you're upset. I'd really appreciate if you could please stop abusing us, and let's try to resolve this together as fairly as possible."

Abuse by a customer isn't only the verbal or physical kind, but also the abuse of guest privilege, as in the case of the lady mentioned above. The money that a customer pays covers the product or service we offer, but not the

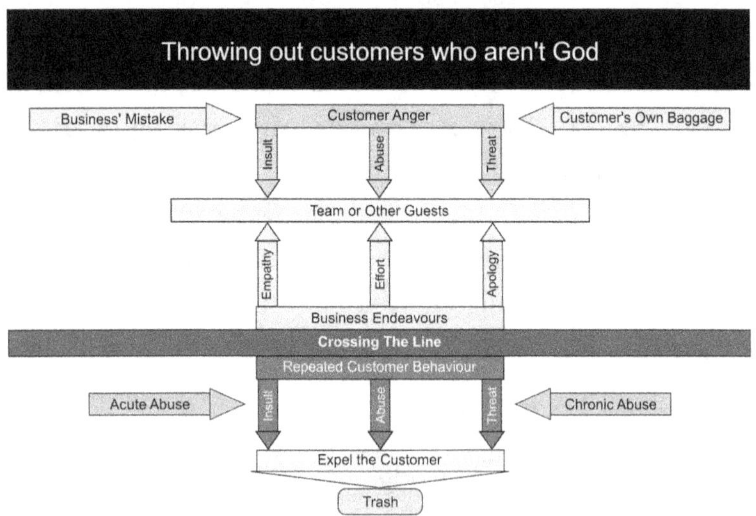

right to abuse. Abuse, in the heat of the moment, may be overlooked and the guest welcomed again, if you so wish.

Unacceptable behaviour

Two types of abuses hurled by a customer must be considered unacceptable and lead to definitive action on your part:

1. Acute abuse—of the strong, one-time, or infrequent kind.
2. Chronic abuse—which happens regularly.

In either case, the very presence of a person indulging in such behaviour results in the release of toxicity towards your team or your other guests, which, of course, is terrible for the business. This is typically the last threshold of tolerance for even the most customer-sensitive establishments.

A customer who continues to misbehave beyond this point may be deemed to have crossed the line of acceptable behaviour and in the interest of the safety and sanctity of your enterprise, it becomes necessary to throw out such a 'God'.

The restaurant business, however gratifying, takes up a lot of time and energy. Those within it who work sincerely, invariably feel drained out from time to time. Over long periods, it may even take a toll on our health and that of our team.

So, here is an especially important piece about weathering difficult times...

Personal Fitness: A Game Changer for Industry Outcomes

The stress of running our family hotel coupled with poor lifestyle habits—from improper rest to a bad diet, claimed my father's life at forty-two. At work, industry seniors did double-shifts for weeks without a break and rarely ate a proper meal on time because my 24/7 operational sector exalted such professionals as 'dedicated'.

We feed our guests and look after their welfare but not our own. It takes a toll by way of burnout, depression, and even death—on an individual, his family, and his work.

Inspiration came from my maternal grandparents, both good swimmers and long-distance cyclists in their early years, incidentally non-vegetarians, who lived healthily into their nineties while continuing to at least walk and stretch every day. On the other hand, I saw colleagues who, rather than blame their long hours and tough schedules, committed time to their health exuding better energy and way better productivity. This is what I wanted for myself and everyone around me.

From an early age, I trained in the National Cadet Corps (NCC), yoga, martial arts, and meditation. These helped me stay anchored through challenges at work and at home. I also learnt other fitness habits from many entrepreneurs, colleagues, and coaches.

Nowadays, we are told that wellness, well-being, fitness, etc., are different things. However, rather than getting into semantics or technical definitions about what represents good health most holistically, I have used them interchangeably in this section, for the sake of ease of understanding.

Here's an approach I find useful in developing one's personal fitness.

The body, mind, and spirit are the three pillars of health through which we face the world. Damage to either one of them diminishes our productivity and can destroy our capacity to meet challenges. A single malfunction here and all our business intellect and capabilities become pointless. Thus, managing this 'system' with our thoughts, words, and actions is of utmost importance.

Thoughts

- Work, however important, as an occupation and income is only a part of life, not all of it.
- Be aware of the stress on account of each aspect of life.
- Plan on-going weekly fitness routines and interim breaks to refresh yourself.
- Know that 'making excuses' is going to cost you and 'finding time' is in your control.
- Disciplined execution of your plan sows the seeds of good health over the long term.
- Good habits can't prevent an illness or accident, but can improve your ability to face them.

Words

Listen to motivational words from others and engage in positive self-talk.

Actions

Pillar 1 - The Body: Exercise, Nourish, and Rest

- Exercise–Regularly train your body for strength, balance, stamina, agility, and flexibility.
- Nourish–Tailor-make your ideal diet based on your situation, observe the feedback your body gives you.
- Rest–Sleep well to rejuvenate.

Pillar 2 - The Mind: Engage

- Learn a new sport, art, or language.
- Practice problem-solving–Work on a big or small puzzle, even if you can't actually solve it.
- Empty your mind's 'recycle bin' frequently.
- Revitalize yourself through entertainment, nothingness, and silence.
- Overcome inertia and procrastination through action.

Pillar 3 - The Spirit: Purpose

- Boost yourself through good relationships and a smile.
- Travel to experience new cultures of people, their history, food, music, etc.
- Help someone less privileged who cannot give you back anything.
- Periodically push yourself outside your comfort zone.
- Relax in nature–climb a mountain, feel a river, pet an animal.

You can choose from a limitless range of activities and an array of experts who can help you.

I personally learned the lesson on substance and personality early on in my life.

I was twenty and had just been rejected at an on-campus job interview at IHM for a management trainee position at the airport outlet of a five-star hotel's flight kitchen. From the line of questioning, it was obvious to me that my appearance was the reason.

I was quite upset that the 'substance' of what I had to offer was overlooked. I spoke to an industry senior about it. He thoughtfully explained that some hospitality jobs, especially guest-facing ones, require an aspect of 'personality', which he felt I could develop.

The chronologically

'Before & After'

PICS I COULD FIND...

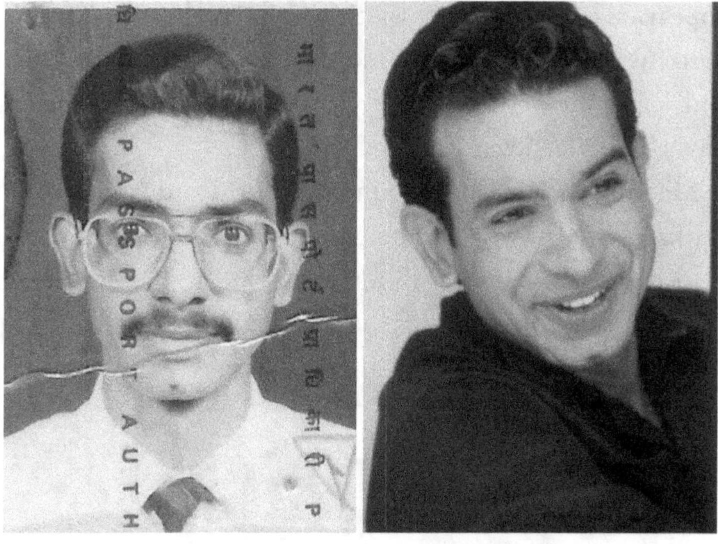

A friend I mentioned this to introduced me to his schoolmate who was a fashion designer and one of India's first male models. One look at me and the stylist said, "Take off your glasses. Hmm, you have a good bone structure. Get yourself some contact lenses, brush your hair back and gel it, and lose the moustache… to start with." When I met him some weeks later, he smiled and nodded: "Not too shabby".

At a time when access to online information on anything (let alone makeovers) was extremely limited, his insights were invaluable, and I felt immensely grateful to him for helping me begin my journey of developing those aspects of myself that I hadn't realized mattered.

The reactions around me were clear. My family and old friends were initially a bit surprised and tickled with my new look, but seemed to like it. The industry community and new people I met, approved as well.

I knew that age or an accident could easily take away my appearance and realized that personality had to be more than just that shell. I explored this in depth over the years and learnt how to be more visible, yet go back to being 'invisible', whenever I needed to.

Meeting people from around the world and from various walks of life has been tremendously rewarding, and has helped me learn more about what we as human beings value on the inside and on the outside.

Now, let's get to the typical sort of issues we must handle on a daily basis.

Handling Challenges

"It's not that I'm so smart, it's just that I stay with problems longer."
– Albert Einstein

Despite having a good operations system, there are always some problems in the running of a restaurant. This chapter will deal with some of the commonest problems faced in a day-to-day situation, internal and external, short-term and long-term, and suggest ways to tackle them.

Analyzing your SWOT:

Involve yourself and your core team in an honest and realistic evaluation of your Strengths, Weaknesses, Opportunities and Threats (SWOT) regularly.

Ask yourself questions from your own and other people's perspective. Then, make a plan of action on how best you could leverage your strengths, overcome your weaknesses, utilize your opportunities, and eliminate your threats.

- Strengths: Your intrinsic advantages or edge in the marketplace.
- Weaknesses: Disadvantages or flaws in your business.
- Opportunities: Market changes (social, political, etc.) that you could use to your advantage, events in your favour (such as trade fairs), or other possibilities like diversification, expansion, mergers and acquisitions.
- Threats: Obstacles that may choke your productivity or existence. They may be either internal (such as an employee issue), or, external (such as a competitor's positioning).

Common problems and their solutions

- Partnership disagreements: Put down the scope of work of each individual partner and reinforce common objectives. If all else fails, buy out your partner or sell your own shareholding. Avoid litigation (settling out of court is almost always cheaper and faster).
- Landlord matters: Expiry and renewal of your agreement, annual rent increases, and other landlord authorizations need to be agreed upon in writing at the onset. A mutual understanding is crucial for harmonious coexistence.
- Licensing problems: Prepare for the red tape and challenges you will face well in advance. Budget for an additional margin of time and money, some of which will be spent on 'speed money'. A compromise must be reached if necessary with a mediator such as an agent, social worker, politician, etc.
- Personal problems leaving you, the proprietor, incapacitated: De-stress yourself and try to delegate more so as to be hands-free. If the situation gets acute, you may need to bring in a partner, shareholders, or even a buyer.
- Neighbourhood trouble: Understand neighbours' grievances and jointly work towards mutually-beneficial solutions. In case of crime, police assistance may be required.
- Bad publicity: Don't wait for this to happen. Proactively study the guest feedback forms to prevent bad publicity. Develop loyalty programs to reinforce

customer relationships. Educate employees and encourage their performance, emphasizing politeness and courtesy to customers.

- Improper supplies: Check contracts for loopholes and look into purchases, receipts, storage, and issue practices.
- Competition woes/declining customer loyalty: A study of the competitor's ongoing innovations and resources can be revealing. Rethinking your overall current strategy and revitalizing your restaurant space could be in order.
- High staff turnover: Deep dive into your HR policies and practices at every step, from candidate screening till exit interviews. Understand your staff's perspective about your establishment and work towards a better retention program.
- Unexpected staff shortage: Everyone present, regardless of hierarchy, will need to pitch in and help out.
- Minor accidents or injuries: Develop standard accident response procedures for employees and guests. Provide staff with first-aid training and information on nearby hospitals, doctors, and insurance coverage. Keep an emergency kit and firefighting equipment on the premises.
- Electricity failure: If you are in an area that has regular power failures, you may need a generator.
- Water shortage: Have an arrangement for a water tanker to be sent at short notice.
- Computer system failure: In case of electric failure,

there could be a provision for a battery back-up (Uninterruptible Power Supply) to allow saving information and an orderly shutdown. A pre-prepared manual system should be available and staff advised on procedures to be followed.

- High electricity bills: Check for energy loss through careless use, high-energy consuming appliances, etc.
- High gas bills: Look at your gas bank connection and revaluate for wastage through leftover gas in cylinders. Check for overuse as well as leaking or misused stopcocks or pipes. Use certified one-way valves and regulators for safety and economy.
- High water bills: Follow the passage of water from source to consumption via storage. Regulate water level and pumping time. Confirm the required quantity. Check for overflow, over consumption, and leakage.
- Food shortage at the buffet counter: Keep your commitment to your guests by buying those dishes readymade immediately if necessary, even from a competitor!
- Excessive leftover food: If the food is not consumable it should be disposed of, otherwise it can be donated to a social cause.

Sound judgement can be compromised by fatigue, hunger, and stress. Being watchful of this helps make better decisions.

For a restaurant to remain interesting and in good health, we need to rejuvenate it from time to time.

Business Rejuvenation and Turnaround

Consumer preferences and demands keep changing. Responding to these changes innovatively and tweaking our business concept accordingly is the only way to stay relevant in the market. The key is to decide what kind of change is required, when, how, and to what extent.

Sharp businessmen anticipate market changes before they actually occur and become known as trendsetters. The rest follow suit, keeping pace with the market while the change occurs. These two categories are considered either good or safe to be in.

If, however, a business is lagging behind the market, it may need rejuvenation to bring it in line with consumer demand. If a business is too far behind, its very survival may be threatened.

The telltale signs of a business in trouble are generally its financial condition and brand perception. Some companies feel that if they are doing well financially, the 'hocus-pocus' of a brand doesn't matter, but they slowly realize that competitors soon copy their business model and the only way to survive the threat is differentiating themselves through their brand. Others become complacent or even smug about their goodwill in the market and soon discover that even great brand equity will not allow them to get away with a mismatch of their offer.

If your business is in such a position, then you need to develop a rejuvenation or turnaround plan that will give you the best likelihood of recovery.

I believe the order of tasks for a rejuvenation or turnaround exercise should be:

1. Finding a Change Agent

Albert Einstein once said, "Insanity is doing the same thing over and over again and expecting different results."

A project 'owner' should be someone dedicated to bring about the required change, rather than being burdened with day-to-day activities. A change agent may be either an external individual or organization like a consultant, or, an internal senior employee or director who can undertake the job of Chief Restructuring Officer (CRO). It would be best to have a combination of both—someone from the outside and someone from the inside working together. In this manner, between the two they will jointly have the technical knowledge, people skills and trust, objectivity, and the drive necessary to conduct the exercise successfully.

2. Assessing the situation

The best place to start assessments is with the people—consumers, employees, vendors, and other business associates.

Consumers would obviously be the purest source of information about your product offer and its present and future relevance in the market. Their perception of your brand and what it stands for in terms of depth and flexibility would be a good indicator of the way forward.

The employees' direct daily contact with the consumer and the business processes can be the basis of identifying gaps in the delivery of your offer. Their mindset, that of their leader (business head), and their relationship with the promoters will also inevitably provide leads for your exercise.

Likewise, you can speak with vendors and other business associates to understand the business from their perspective.

Subsequently, you should look inward at the company's practices, processes, and policies and seek opportunities to improve efficiencies. For instance, an extensive menu that is not practical to manage can be reduced or altered, or an existing inadequate management information system can be improved.

Essentially, the assessment exercise must bring to the forefront the company's strengths, weaknesses, opportunities, and threats. It will form the basis of our business plan.

While speaking with these various parties, one must remember that each of their views on the same aspect of the business might be different. Sometimes it may even be contrary to that of the promoter's perspective. This is where the objectivity of 'What is in the best interest of the business?' can be our guiding light and must be kept sacred.

3. Developing a business plan

Having collected all the relevant information, the change agents must analyze it and develop a holistic plan. Since we have cited financial condition and brand perception as indicators of the company's health, these could be our scoreboards. You thus need to list out all possible initiatives that might help.

So, how you can increase sales, reduce costs, and present your revised offer to the market, should be on the agenda. You must thoroughly analyze and discuss your internal processes to bring about practical efficiencies.

Customers' habits and preferences are an important consideration, as they may indicate which 'yes' button you can press that might persuade them to choose your brand over others.

If you are short on staff skills, training may fill the gap. Alternatively, if new blood is required, existing employees may become concerned about their job security. Therefore, a communication plan to existing employees explaining the needs of the business is critical to maintain harmony in the organization.

Generally, by using Pareto's 80:20 principle, you could focus on the significant few (in this case, issues and initiatives) versus the insignificant many. Accordingly, some areas will need to be retained or ramped up while others may need to be amputated.

At this stage, you will conclude what core changes are necessary, when, how, and to what extent. You must be fully aware of which decisions are reversible and which are not.

Some decisions that initially seem irreversible may, in fact, be reversible. For example, if you are locked into a rent agreement, which is burdensome to you but great for the landlord, you could have a go at renegotiating terms. While he may not be keen to revise the arrangement, he may, for instance, view your reliable payment schedule and tenacity favourably in a high tenant turnover market.

To successfully execute your plan, you will need to nominate 'initiative owners' who will drive the initiatives as intended.

4. Executing the plan

The success of any plan is inevitably in the execution. Taking the staff into confidence and sharing your new vision with clarity is, therefore, the key to achieve your targets. Employee buy-in is critical to the progress of any initiatives in an organization. This buy-in will come only when the management tangibly acts upon their opinion. When you act on staff recommendations, you effectively renew their morale and ownership of the brand.

Furthermore, the staff must be encouraged to discuss their recommendations on the business plan as well as voice their needs that are not being currently met by the business. The two can be linked in a manner that conveys the co-relation between business and employee benefit.

Training them in skills would enhance their qualities to a higher level than they currently possess. This would not only increase their market value, but may also be an added incentive. The better they understand the reasons for specific initiatives being taken, the more likely they are to contribute productively toward this exercise. Provoke professional pride in employees that have it and cultivate it in those that do not.

Clarify your expectations from your team, discuss timeframes and implications of the success and failure of the plan both on the business as as well on everyone involved.

Seeing this exercise through requires a high level of focus and energy that is sustained by a strong will and backed by the necessary resources. Decisions once taken must be followed through with action.

Rather than attribute blame to people, the organization as a whole must agree on the single-minded approach to destroy anything that blocks the path to the company's progress.

Ensuring good leadership and aligning team initiatives with the plan, gradually leads to prioritization of the right tasks becoming second nature.

On occasion, during your exercise, you may encounter challenges even greater than those the business directly has to offer. Therefore, issues like co-promoter rigidity, union agendas, etc., may render even a first-class business plan ineffective and lead to failure. But try you must.

5. Creating an ongoing monitoring and communication system

Knowing about the ongoing successes and failures of each initiative is something all employees who have invested themselves in this exercise would like to know. Therefore, you must devise and maintain a regular monitoring and communicating mechanism that conveys results and shares information on customer satisfaction and financial achievement.

I find the 'balanced scorecard' a useful framework within which we can effectively create, implement, and measure the success of our strategy from four perspectives:

a) **Financial:** Return on investment, profitability, sales, and costs.
b) **Customer:** Market share, customer retention, customer acquisition, and customer satisfaction.
c) **Employee growth and learning:** Satisfaction, retention, and productivity.
d) **Internal processes:** Unique key processes based on adding value for the customer.

Looking at these metrics and tracking and diagnosing them will help us take well-informed decisions.

If your business is facing a crisis and you're wondering whether or not your team will be open to such an exercise, do remember that when confronted with survival issues even a team that has rigidity hardwired into its DNA will recognize and respond to the need for change… or die.

So, at regular intervals, all businesses, like individuals, inevitably come across demons that they must confront and overcome.

My Formula for Your Success

Everyone wants a magic formula for success and, as you know, there never really is one. But the closest I will wager on is this…

A Clear Plan
+ Effective action
+ Flexibility (based on listening to your customers)
+ Blessings of all stakeholders
+ Good timing
+ Luck

= Restaurant success!

If you keep an eye on each of these components and work on them continually, you will greatly improve your chances of success. Never forget that all this can only be achieved if you pay close attention to your health and pace yourself out over the long term. Only then, can you come back refreshed enough the next day, to serve your guests with a fresh mind and clean heart.

The most effective way to reduce your risk is to always stay on top of the needs and wants of your guests. You can do this simply by asking them and also by deeply studying their habits and preferences. The better you do this and keep tweaking your value proposition accordingly, the more aligned and relevant you will be to the ever-evolving demands of your audience.

Be nimble and move with the times by constantly Differentiating, Innovating and Evolving; or else your business will become irrelevant and DIE.

A classic mistake wealthy entrepreneurs make in their restaurant start-up is to hire experienced professionals while they remain employed elsewhere or running other businesses. This is much like paying an annual gym membership, not putting in the time themselves, and hoping they will get fit. This, in fact, is a sure way to lose your investment in this sector.

To lead and succeed in the restaurant business, you must first learn it, not just theoretically, but practically, on the job. The food business is the people business and the only way to learn it and manage it is to invest time with your people... your customers, your team, and your associates.

When taking decisions, it is important to listen to your people objectively and then consciously decide when to override their viewpoints or when to override your own.

When you put money down in this business, be sure to put down your time behind it as well. Otherwise, you will always blame yourself for not giving it your best shot.

I find that not every restaurant that succeeds delivers excellence on all fronts from day one. But if you can do well enough on most fronts, to the extent that your customers will be willing to forgive your early mistakes long enough for you to survive, you will have a solid chance of victory over the long term.

If you can show your patrons that you truly listen, always act upon their complaints, and often on their suggestions as well, the marketplace will reward you (financially and otherwise) with a deep sense of pride and achievement, that only a restaurateur can know.

All my very best for your endeavour!

Glossary

86'd: When an item on the menu is unavailable for sale, it is referred to as 86'd. A drunk customer or even an exhausted colleague is also deemed to be 86'd.

À la, Au/Aux: French terms referring to the style or manner of cooking, or what the dish is served with. For example, café au lait meaning coffee with milk or tarte aux pommes meaning apple tart.

À la Carte: A type of menu where each item is separately listed, described, and priced.

À la Minut: Referring to a dish cooked to order.

Al Dente: Literally means 'to the teeth/to the bite'. The term is used when evaluating the correct degree of doneness of dishes, particularly vegetables and pasta. It is considered just right when biting into an item offers a slight resistance without being hard.

Al Fresco: Literally translated 'in the fresh air', this term in the restaurant industry refers to outdoor dining spaces.

American Service: American style food service involves serving restaurant guests food that is pre-plated in the kitchen itself. Table sauces, Bread and Butter, Salads, etc., are usually placed at the table. Possibly the only style of food service wherein service is from the right side of the guest.

Amortise: When a business gradually writes off the initial costs of its assets or repays its loan regularly over a period of time, it is said to be amortising the capital costs or loan.

Angel Investor: An investor who provides capital and sometimes even guidance to start-up businesses in return for a shareholding or equity in the company. Considering the risk they take in first-time entrepreneurial ventures, they usually expect high returns. Referring to them as 'angels', might just stem from the fact that they invest at a stage prior to proof of concept.

Apéritif: An alcoholic drink taken as an appetizer before a meal.

Appetizer: A small portion of food or beverage taken before a meal to stimulate the appetite.

Asset Register: A register that lists the restaurant's assets, including land, building, machinery, and equipment, their purchase date, purchase price and a few details necessary to compute the depreciation and tax on these items. It also helps keep track of smaller items such as furniture, computers, etc., and their physical condition during internal audits conducted usually by the Finance and Accounts department.

ATL: 'Above the Line' refers to sales and marketing techniques that promote the awareness of a brand through media channels, including television, radio, print, cinema, the internet, and even out-of-home mediums like billboards. Since the agencies involved used to charge a commission when the phrase was created, accountants back then categorized them as 'operating expenses' and therefore called them 'above the line' costs.

Audit: An examination of stocks, systems, or processes such as inventory management, financial transactions, customer experiences, etc., to check for theft, or, the need to improve systems.

Average bill per head: The total sales per day divided by the total number of visitors that day.

B&B plate: Bread and Butter plate is a six-inch side plate placed to the left of the dinner plate. In a fine dining restaurant, it would be used to place bread to be buttered and consumed. It is also known as a quarter plate and in many cases side dishes or starters are placed in it for consumption.

Back burner: As putting a pot on the back burner implies that it isn't actively being attended to, just simmering, so also tasks put on the back burner would be the ones that are low priority for the moment.

Back of the house: Usually consists of the office, kitchen, stores, and dish washing area.

Bain-Marie: A water bath or double boiler that comprises two utensils: a smaller one placed inside a larger one with a liquid (usually water) in between. A warm bain-marie (with hot water) may be used for cooking custards, melting chocolate, etc., or for keeping food warm as with chaffing dishes on buffet counters. A cold bain-marie (with cold water) may be used for whipping cream, mousses, etc., or for keeping food cold as in the case of a salad counter.

Barista: Italian for bartender, a Barista is a person proficient in the art of preparing and pulling espresso-based and other beverages at a coffee shop or any other type of restaurant.

BCG Matrix: A four-quadrant tool for restaurant menu engineering, named after a business consulting firm called the Boston Consulting Group where it was first created. Each item on the menu is mapped to two parameters: profitability and popularity.

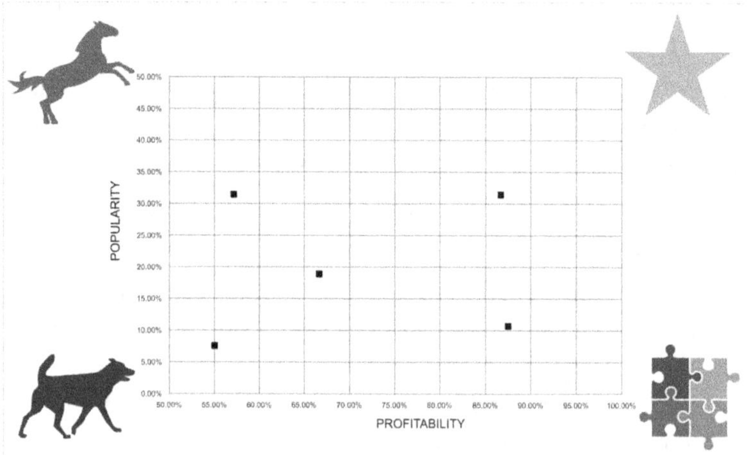

* Diagram: BCG Matrix

The standardized recipe card provides us with details on profitability (selling price minus recipe cost) while the POS data provides us with the number of units sold per dish, indicating its popularity.

1. Stars (High Popularity and High Profitability) are the best menu items, usually signature dishes to be up-sold.

2. Plowhorses (High Popularity but Low Profitability) with their selling price slightly increased could become stars, thus bettering business.

3. Puzzles (Low Popularity but High Profitability) are difficult to sell, sometimes even if their selling price is reduced. It may be worth considering altering the taste, presentation or name of the dish, with a view to enhancing its popularity. If unsuccessful, treat as a dog.

4. Dogs (Low Popularity and Low Profitability) are difficult to sell, and if sold, offer little profit. Thus these are best eliminated from the menu.

Bev Nap: A 'beverage napkin' which collects the condensed droplets on a beverage glass. A small square napkin is either placed on the table below the glass as a coaster or a long rectangular one is wrapped around the glass when offering it to a guest.

Bill/Check: Item-wise total of purchases along with service charge and taxes.

Biometrics: Verifying the identity of individuals using features like fingerprints to allow limited access to confidential data and at a more basic level to authenticate the presence of a staff member on duty, which is then linked to his salary disbursement, leave, etc.

Birth purpose: The reason why an employee has been hired, usually his core competence for the job.

Bistro: A small informal restaurant serving slow-cooked food at moderate prices; meals along with wine.

Blast chiller/freezer: A blast chiller is a commercial appliance usually used by restaurants and catering companies to rapidly cool down food from 70°C to 3°C or lower in around 90 minutes, thereby, rendering it safe for storage and future consumption, for instance, when chilling wine. A blast freezer is similar, but takes the temperature down even further to −18°C in around 240 minutes, for instance for freezing ice cream.

BLT: Bacon, Lettuce, and Tomato sandwich made with mayonnaise, is a popular sandwich in the US and UK.

BOGO: 'Buy one get one free' is a promotional offer at restaurants and other retail businesses. For instance, during lean hours at a restaurant, you may offer a free pint of beer for every pint bought.

BOQ: The Bill of Quantities is an itemized statement of the cost components, including materials and labour, of a project during construction. It serves as the basis of comparison for competitive bids between potential contractors and also a frame of reference to measure actual itemized costs and quantities versus those budgeted.

Bottom Line: Profit or Loss, which is the bottom item of a profit and loss statement and the final outcome of importance to a business.

Boulangerie: A French-style bakery that specialises in baking and selling bread.

Bouquet Garni: An assortment of either fresh or dried herbs used to enhance the flavour of stocks, stews, soups, casseroles and broths. They may either be wrapped inside a cheesecloth or muslin sachet and then placed in the stock, or simply tied together and placed in it directly. For example, in French cuisine, it may include parsley, rosemary, thyme, and peppercorns.

Breakeven: The point where the business expenses equal the income generated, with neither profit nor loss.

Broth: A thin soup made from meat or fish stock.

Busboy/Busser: An assistant waiter who helps lay out tables, clear dirty dishes, and supports the service experience, usually with less direct guest contact than the waiter.

BTL: 'Below the Line' refers to those sales and marketing techniques that are more focused and measurable, using mediums such as direct mailers, flyers, telemarketing, stickers, point of sale brochures, exhibitions, etc. Since no commission was involved when the phrase was created, accountants back then categorized them as 'capital expenditure' and, therefore, called them 'below the line' costs.

Business model: The way in which an organization creates and delivers value to its customers and attracts them to pay for that value in a manner that results in a profit.

BYOB: 'Bring Your Own Bottle' is a restaurant policy that allows guests to bring their own liquor. It is often subject to a fee known as 'corkage'.

CAC: Customer Acquisition Cost is the cost of acquiring a new customer. It is a metric that every business owner or leader should know. Convincing each additional customer about the value of your product involves initiatives in research as well as sales and marketing. So, for instance, if all these costs add up to say ₹30,000/- for a certain period and you have acquired say 100 new customers in that period, then your cost of acquiring each new customer, i.e., CAC will be 30,000/100 = ₹300/-.

Café: Synonymous with coffee shop, a café usually refers to a small restaurant where snacks or light meals are served with drinks which may also include alcoholic beverages.

CAGR: Compounded Annual Growth Rate is a term representing the year-on-year growth of a business investment over a specified period of time.

Cambro: A US-based restaurant-ware company renowned for its food and beverage storage containers which keep hot food hot and cold food cold. Nowadays, the word Cambro is often used synonymously with any brand of plastic storage containers.

Cannibalization: It refers to the loss of a restaurant's market share in a particular catchment on account of a similar offer coming up in that catchment, either by another outlet of the same brand or by a competitor.

Capex: Capital expenditure is the amount spent towards the procurement of assets that increase the capacity or efficiency of a business for more than one accounting year. Assets include building, equipment, vehicles, etc.

Cash flow: The movement of money into and out of a business that affects its liquidity. It is a measure of financial efficiency.

Casual dining: A restaurant which offers a casual ambience and food at moderate prices where formal dressing is unnecessary. Table service usually involves food being served either pre-plated or on platters, with or without a buffet option.

CCG: Cutlery, Crockery, Glassware is easy to refer to in one cluster as CCG in the Restaurant Business.

CDP / DCDP: Chef de Partie / Demi Chef de Partie is a chef in charge of a particular section in the kitchen such as grills, sauces, etc. In standalone restaurants, he may have a wider responsibility than handling just one section. He is the third in-charge of the kitchen, the first being the head/executive chef and the second being the sous/under chef.

Chaffing dish: A dish of stainless steel or silver with a heating device fitted below it to keep food warm over an extended period of time, such as on a buffet.

Charcuterie: A charcuterie is a specialized store or a space within a hotel dedicated to the cooking, curing and smoking of meats, mainly pork as well as others, including game meats, game birds, poultry, veal and seafood. Products on offer are essentially served cold and usually include sausages, pâtés, terrines, galantines, roulades, etc.

Chaser: A drink that immediately follows another drink. For instance, a beer after a straight shot of hard liquor.

Chef's table: A table at a restaurant that offers an exclusive meal experience to discerning guests, usually for a premium price. The table is located either in the kitchen itself or right next to it, while the chef prepares his culinary creations.

COD: Cash On Delivery. Referring to payment terms agreed upon between vendor and client.

COGs: Cost of Goods sold. In the case of food and beverage, for instance, it would include not just the materials used to produce that particular category of food and beverage, but also materials 'consumed' through wastage, spoilage, theft, or complementaries, thereby allowing one to keep a tab on actual versus budgeted COGs.

Combi-oven: A combination oven which offers three cooking modes for a versatile range of cooking processes:

1. Convection mode—using dry air for baking cookies, frying potato wedges, or roasting chicken.

2. Steam mode—using moist air for steaming vegetables or poaching fish.

3. Combination mode—using both moist and dry air for stewing fruit or braising meat.

Commis: A junior kitchen assistant or apprentice who performs the more basic tasks of food production in each section of the kitchen, getting promoted from Commis III to Commis II and finally to Commis I, before reaching a DCDP level.

Commissary: A kitchen facility where food is prepared for distribution to multiple locations. It could be a centralized space where food is partly prepared for a chain of restaurants where the final cooking is completed. It may also be a place where food is entirely prepared and then delivered, either to other eateries where it is sold, or directly to customers as in a catering service.

Comp off: A compensatory off given to a restaurant employee for having worked on his holiday.

Comping: Comping a meal or dish means giving it free or complimentary to a guest who may either be a regular patron, one of some commercial importance to the establishment, or even one whose experience at our restaurant has not been up to the mark.

Controlling interest: A shareholder who owns over 50% of a company's voting shares, may be deemed to have 'controlling interest' in the company. At times, when the shareholding may be even less than 50%, but the remaining shares are not actively voted, the shareholder may also have effective control of the company.

Corkage: Restaurants that allow guests to bring their own alcohol, may levy a charge called corkage for consuming liquor (originally drawing the cork of each bottle of wine, now other liquor as well) bought 'off the restaurant premises'.

Cost of capital: If the capital is your own, then how much interest would it have earned in another investment? If you are taking a loan, then how much interest are you paying?

Cost-centre: A department within an organization which does not contribute to its profits, but instead only adds to its costs, is called a cost-centre. In a restaurant for instance, departments like human resources, marketing, accounts, IT and admin are examples of cost-centres since they come with a cost attached, but don't bring in any profit directly. Their presence, however, is pivotal to improving the efficiency of the organization at large and boosting its productivity. Such 'cost-centres' are therefore a necessary part of the business.

Cover/Covers: Refers to (a) the table setting laid out for a single guest or (b) the number of guests that can be seated in the restaurant.

Cover charge: A fixed charge levied for a place at a table, in addition to the charge for food and beverage.

Creditor days: A ratio that tells us how many days on average it takes a company to pay for the goods or services it buys. In the restaurant industry, depending on the terms we have finalized with each of our vendors, we must make our payments. If a certain vendor allows us a 30-day credit period and we pay him late, say in 45 days, it will strain the relationship. At the same time, paying up too early doesn't allow us the use of good cash flow for our working capital.

If in a certain period the restaurant owes its vendors ₹9,00,000/- and our cost of sales for that period is ₹150,00,000/-, then the creditor days of the restaurant will be = ₹9,00,000 / ₹150,00,000 × 365 days = 21.9 days. Creditor Days = Trade Credit / Cost of Sales × 365 days.

Cross-contamination: The unintentional transfer of bacteria or other microorganisms through hands, clothes, or kitchen tools from a food or non-food source with harmful human effect.

Crumbing: In the kitchen, the term 'crumbing' or 'breading' refers to coating a piece of wet food with a bread-like mixture such as bread crumbs before cooking. In the restaurant, the term 'crumbing' refers to clearing the table of food crumbs between courses, with the help of a small brush.

CTC: Cost To Company is the total annual cost that a company incurs towards retaining a particular employee. It includes all expenses which are a part of the salary as well as perks and other hidden expenses which may not be a part of the remuneration package. Ideally it should include the cost of items which directly or indirectly go towards an employee's gain such as training programs for instance but not the cost of business-related expenses such as mobile phone bills incurred to conduct the company's business. This interpretation of CTC varies from organization to organization.

Culinarian: A person who cooks or is associated with culinary arts.

Damask: A reversible fabric used for table covers or even curtains made of linen or silk with a pattern woven into it.

Dashboard report: A management tool that measures and presents critical data on the key business performance areas in a summarized manner much like a car dashboard so management can quickly respond.

Debtor days: A ratio that tells us how many days on average it takes a company to get paid for what it sells. In the restaurant industry, though we get paid for dine-in sales by cash/credit card immediately, delayed payments sometimes occur in party catering. For example, if a customer owes the restaurant ₹ 3,00,000/- and our sales for that period is ₹ 150,00,000/-, then the debtor days of the restaurant at that time will be = ₹ 3,00,000 / ₹ 150,00,000 × 365 days = 7.3 days. Debtor Days = Trade Debt / Sales × 365 days. In a restaurant business, since we don't really need to offer credit to anyone, zero debtor days would be ideal.

Delicatessen: Sometimes abbreviated to 'deli', a delicatessen is a store that sells fine foods like cured meats, pickled vegetables, artisanal cheeses and ice creams, ethnic dips, etc., to the luxury market. Some delis also have a sit-down restaurant section where sandwiches, salads, cold pressed juices, rotisserie chicken, gourmet coffees, etc., may be served.

Depreciation: Writing off the value of an asset over the period of its useful life.

Designated driver: To ensure a safe drive home for his companions from a social event, one person elects to abstain from alcohol himself. Some bars offer an incentive of free non-alcoholic beverages to these 'designated drivers' thereby encouraging social responsibility as well as their own sales of liquor. These days, for everyone in the group to have fun, designated drivers maybe simply be outsourced to a paid-for agency.

Due diligence: The detailed investigation of a business or person before transacting with them. For instance, you may conduct legal, financial, and operational due diligence of a business before you consider buying that business, or verifying facts about a certain individual before entering into a contract with him.

EBITDA: Earnings Before Interest, Taxes, Depreciation and Amortization.

EMI: Equated Monthly Instalment is the method by which one can pay back a loan in terms of both the principal as well as the interest amount.

English Service: A formal sort of food service in which the host or hostess flamboyantly carves or portions out meat or vegetable dishes on the platters in which they are served. Then, the waiter takes these platters around to first serve the guest of honour, followed by the remaining guests.

Entrées: The course following the fish course in a French classical menu. Generally, well-garnished and served with a gravy or sauce.

Equity: Net worth of an organization comprising of paid up equity capital plus reserves and surplus.

ERP: Enterprise Resource Planning is a business management system which integrates various activities of the business. In a restaurant, activities include Food Production, Inventory Management, HR, Marketing, Finance and Accounts, Customer Database, etc.

ESOP: An Employee Stock Option Plan is a method of compensating employees with shares of the company rather than only a cash salary for their work. It encourages a culture of loyalty and reduces the outgoing cash burden on the business. The company typically buys back stocks from the employee only when he leaves or retires. ESOPs also bring the advantage of reduced tax burdens.

EV: Enterprise Value is a measure of a company's value—often the theoretical price in the event of a buyout. It considers not just the equity of the company but also its debt (since the buyer will have to assume it) and its cash (which the buyer will receive). Debt increases the buying cost of the company, while cash reduces it. It is usually expressed as a multiple of either the Last Twelve Months (LTM) Revenue or its EBITDA.

In highly mature markets like the US, restaurants may see a Median EV of say 0.9 to 2.1 times LTM Revenue or say 7.7 to 9.9 times LTM EBITDA, depending on the type of restaurant: Fine Dining / Casual Dining / Quick Service, etc., ("Restaurant Industry Insights" – Duff and Phelps). In less mature markets like India, which have much more room for growth, EVs are often higher.

Exhaust: The ventilation system comprising of ducting and exhaust fans that facilitate the inflow of fresh air and the outflow of hot/stale air.

Eyeballs: In a marketing context, eyeballs refer to the number of people that will see the promotional material of your company brand.

FAQs: Frequently Asked Questions.

Feasibility study: A tool that helps evaluate the positive and negative aspects of a business opportunity, study the risks, and identify ways to mitigate them, before committing an investment and taking an informed decision on its technical, social and financial viability.

FF&E: Furniture, Fixtures, and Equipment. Movable furniture and heavy equipment, including tables, chairs, sideboards, computers, refrigerators, cooking ranges, coffee machines, microwave ovens, food processors, worktables, storage racks, etc.

FIFO: First-In, First-Out is a method of inventory management based on the premise that goods bought first (first-in) are the goods sold first (first-out). This is logical from the stores perspective in the case of perishable goods as well as from the accounts perspective since during inflation it yields the best value of closing inventory (the cost of goods bought first, thus cheapest, correspond best with cost of goods sold first).

Financial performance: A representation of the monetary health of a company.

Fire It: Firing a certain dish or the entire order at a particular table is a call for action to actually begin cooking those items immediately. A server estimates the time within which a guest must be served his food as well as the time it would take the kitchen to execute the order and gives a "fire it" request accordingly.

Fit-out: An architectural term in regard to the act of filling the raw shell of a space with a restaurant's interiors, including its ducting, utilities, treatment of walls, floor and ceiling, ventilation, lighting, plumbing, etc.

Float: A small sum of money set aside at the beginning of a period for petty cash expenses.

Focus group discussions: A form of market research where a small group of 8 to 10 people may be brought together and led by a moderator to discuss their opinions, preferences, beliefs and attitudes towards certain products or services, with a view to have a qualitative insight into a small section of the brand's target market.

Food contamination: The unintended presence of harmful substances (physical/chemical/biological) that can cause illnesses such as food poisoning. In some cases, people intentionally use adulterants in food to reduce costs and make a profit.

Food poisoning: An acute illness caused by the consumption of contaminated food usually accompanied by vomiting, fever, aches and even diarrhoea.

Footfall: The number of people frequenting a restaurant or a specific locality, during a particular period of time. Visible footfall at a particular location is often a key consideration in guesstimating possible sales of a business when selecting that location for a start-up.

FQ1, FQ2, FQ3, FQ4: An accounting period of 12 months is broken down into 4 Fiscal Quarters with the business performance measured for each quarter. The fiscal year maybe Jan-Dec, Apr-Mar or otherwise.

Franchise: A business scaling-up technique where the learnings from one unit can successfully be used to grow the brand to multiple units. The concept owner is the franchisor, while the entity investing in the brand is the franchisee. The franchisor earns a one-time fee or royalty from the franchisee for use of the brand name and guidance on the business. The franchisor also earns an ongoing percentage of sales and profit for on-going training and support given to the franchisee.

French Press: Also known as a 'plunger pot', this coffee brewing device may occasionally be used as a tea infuser as well. Coarsely ground coffee is left to steep with water for a few minutes after which it is pushed to the bottom of the device using the plunger. A French Press brings out great flavour in a beverage, but the water needs to be exceedingly hot for the drink to be perfectly satisfying. French pressed coffee or tea left to stand for beyond a few minutes turns bitter and is best consumed soon after pressing the plunger.

French Service: Food salvers are first placed on the guest table. The finishing of the partly cooked food may be done by the waiter on a cart near the dining table itself right before the guest. Then the salvers are returned to the table and the guests help themselves.

Front of the house: Guest visible areas, including the lobby, dining room, and show kitchen if any.

Garde Manger: In French, it translates 'keep to eat'. Essentially a part of the cold kitchen, this section covers pantry items such as soups, salads, sandwiches, sauces, condiments, cheeses, sausages, pâtés, terrines, pickled foods and even ice carvings.

GN pan: Gastronorm Pans are food storage containers used in the food service industry. They are made from food grade stainless steel, polycarbonate or polypropylene.

Goodwill: Often used synonymously with reputation of a business, from an accounting perspective, the goodwill of a business refers to the value of its intangible assets. Typically, the future economic benefits of a business are computed using its present popularity and existing profits as an indicator of its valuation.

Gourmand: A person whose love for food and beverage edges into over-indulgence or gluttony.

Gourmet: A person who cultivates a discerning palate for the appreciation of good food and beverage. At times, an "excessive refinement" borders on elitism.

Grease trap: A plumbing device that intercepts grease such as waste oil and fat present in sinks, dishwashers and cooking equipment and traps it before it blocks the municipal sewer system.

Griddle: A flat metal surface on top of a stove on which food is cooked.

GST: Goods and services tax is a tax levied by the central and state governments, on the suppliers of goods and services. Restaurants in India are categorized based on certain criteria to determine the tax rate. For instance, currently those in certain locations and below a certain turnover, fall under the 5% GST rate, with no option to claim input tax credit (ITC) while others come under the 18% GST rate, with ITC claims.

Gueridon service: An interactive and flamboyant form of restaurant service where food is prepared on a well-equipped trolley or small table in full view of the guest, right next to his table and served to him directly.

HACCP: Hazard Analysis and Critical Control Point is a system that monitors the production, storage and distribution of food with a view to identify and control contamination that could lead to health hazards.

High street: The commercial centre of a city where shops and institutions are located. In the restaurant context, it refers to an independent location where potential guests conducting their business just outside the restaurant doors are likely to step in and patronize the restaurant. Since it is positioned directly on the street, it is less influenced by the success or failure of another business (as may be the case in a mall). Many consider it more desirable than a store-in-store location, particularly for a start-up wishing to start their brand with a clean slate.

Holding time (food):   The amount of time you can hold a dish after it is prepared, until the time it may be served without compromising on the quality and safety of the food. It also applies to the holding of raw food. Whether you are holding raw food or cooked food, ideal hold temperature plays a crucial role in food safety of the dish.

Holding time (table):   The amount of time you can hold a booked table for a late guest, from his reservation time till the time you need to release that table to another guest.

House brand: An item of merchandise declared by an establishment as preferred for its guests and usually offered at a bargain price. For instance, a house brand of wine at a restaurant is one either chosen from those available in the market, or one specially made in-house for them.

HR: Human Resources. Either used to refer to a company's workforce or with regards to the HR department which manages their concerns.

HVAC: Heating, Ventilating, and Air-Conditioning are crucial to the environmental comfort and operational ease of the restaurant and its kitchen.

In-depth interviews: A qualitative market research interview with a single respondent, to detect her motivations, attitudes, and thoughts on the subject of study.

In-house restaurant: A restaurant situated within a larger establishment such as a hotel or corporate office. Unlike a stand-alone restaurant, support functions are shared with the parent organization.

In the weeds: A restaurant team member's plea of being snowed over with so much work, that it's hard to keep up.

Ingress/Egress: The right to enter a property such as a restaurant, is referred to as ingress. A guest who has created an issue in the past for instance, may be denied ingress to the restaurant. The right to leave a property such as a restaurant, is referred to as egress. A guest who is creating an issue in the present may be denied egress from the restaurant.

Inorganic growth: A business plan that involves accelerated growth by merging with or acquiring other businesses is referred to as inorganic growth. Such growth can bring new ideas into the business and also allow quick access to new markets.

IRR: Internal Rate of Return is a budgeting tool to evaluate the attractiveness of return on capital investment in a certain project. It is the annualized effective compounded return rate that makes the Net Present Value of all cash flows from that investment, equal to zero. If the IRR of a project is higher than the return any other investment opportunities offer, then it is desirable to go ahead with the undertaking.

Intellectual Property (IP): An intangible asset of human knowledge that is patented or copyrighted as property of the person or organization who has commissioned or funded the research of such an endeavour. Examples may include the creation of a particular brand-name, a certain formula, a process design innovation, a newly invented piece of equipment, a fresh body of work, etc. On account of the value attached to the creation of this distinctive information, it is considered ethical for parties exposed to such information, to keep it a secret. They are often asked to sign a Non-Disclosure Agreement (NDA) with the IP owner as protection from plagiarism.

Julienne: A knife technique which involves cutting vegetables into thin, even-sized matchsticks. Salads, fries, and garnishes often call for a Julienne cut.

JV: A Joint Venture is a contractual arrangement between two or more parties agreeing to create a new business entity by contributing equity, exercising control over the enterprise, and sharing profits or losses over a finite period of time.

Key money: In parts of a city where the rent act restricts escalation in rentals, landlords protect themselves by collecting additional money from prospective tenants who would like to secure, modify or renew their tenancy. It is usually paid by way of a deposit of some months' rent, often in cash. While in some instances, it is refundable and stated to cover non-payment of rent or damage to property, it is often taken as non-refundable to cover cleaning and repairs. Key Money is illegal in many countries and so though some refer to it as 'goodwill' to protect landlords from below market rentals, others say it is simply a bribe that landlords extract from tenants.

Kill it: Cooking a dish extra-well to the point of almost being burnt. For instance, a guest who emphatically insists that his steak not be the slightest bit pink and wants it really well-done, might be a candidate for his server telling the kitchen that the dish be cremated.

Kitchen steward: One who supports the kitchen staff by keeping all kitchen areas, equipment, and utensils clean and sanitised. Apart from cleaning pots and pans, a kitchen steward would also be responsible for clearing the debris from serviceware, including cutlery, crockery and glasses, and washing them thereafter.

Lead time: The time it takes a vendor/supplier to execute and deliver an order from the time the order is placed. Knowing the lead time helps plan ordering and stocking of supplies.

LCV/CLV: Lifetime Customer Value/Customer Lifetime Value is an assessment of the financial value of a customer to an organization through the entire period of their association.

Example 1: A customer spends ₹100 on each visit, visits once a month and is transferred to another city after 2 years. This customer's lifetime spend will be = ₹100 × 1 time × 24 months = ₹2,400.

Example 2: A customer spends ₹100 on each visit twice a month and continues being a customer for 5 years. This customer's lifetime spend will be = ₹100 × 2 times × 60 months = ₹12,000.

Clearly, all customers are not built equal. (Some customers may even refer you to new ones, without you spending any money in acquiring them). We must also consider the customers that leave. Let's say that out 100 new customers you acquire in a particular month, 5 leave. So the churn rate is 5% per month. This means that the 'lifetime' of your customer will be 1/0.05 = 20 months.

LCV = (Average spend per month × Gross Margin %) / Churn Rate. So if the average spend per month is 150/-, the gross margin 70% and the churn rate 5%, the LCV = (150 × 70%) / 5% = ₹2,100 over 20 months.

LCV to CAC Ratio: When the cost of acquiring a customer exceeds the ability to monetise that customer, the business model is a failure. This ratio helps keep track of just that. If the LCV equals the CAC, it's not worth it. When the LCV is 3 or 4 times the CAC its considered to be a good and sustainable model. If it's two times or less, the business should explore the possibility of spending more on its research as well as sales and marketing initiatives to acquire new customers.

LDA: Legal Drinking Age is the minimum age at which a person is legally permitted to consume alcoholic beverages. Some European countries permit drinking of alcohol from childhood within their home, while some Islamic countries and a few Indian states do not permit it at all. Broadly, across most countries, legal drinking age ranges between 18 and 21 years.

LIFO: While Last-In, First-Out has accounting connotations, in the restaurant business this method of human resource management may be used in the event of a staff lay-off where the employee last hired (Last-In) would be the first to be relieved (First-Out).

Line cook: A line cook is one responsible for looking after a particular line or section of responsibilities in the kitchen. He may be assigned the task of stacking plates at the pick-up counter, cleaning the cooking surfaces of his station, prepping sauces at the snack counter, or cooking food at the grill section on a particular day. Some cooks stay in this position through their career, while for others it is something they may choose at the start of their career as a path to become all-rounders by working each section of the kitchen.

LOI/MOU: Letter of Intent/Memorandum of Understanding is a document that outlines a broad agreement between two or more parties. The extent to which this is legally binding depends on the wording as well as the intention of the parties concerned. It serves as an interim 'in principle' arrangement before a final agreement or contract is signed.

Loss leader: A pricing strategy where a certain dish on the menu is deliberately priced equal to or lower than its actual cost, thereby 'losing' money for the organization. This is done with the intent of 'leading' customers to make other purchases within the business that will bring in the profit; thus the name. For instance, a restaurant may offer a soft serve ice cream at a throw away price, only to encourage its customers to spend more on other items like burgers, which are profitable.

Loyalty program: With a view to retain valuable existing customers and encourage new ones to make frequent purchases, a business creates a reward program through which it awards its guests bonus points, gifts or special services for their patronage to encourage them to continue spending more. The company running the program gains access to their customers' habits and preferences, and other information useful for marketing.

M&A: Mergers and Acquisitions is a phrase used in the context of business strategy where a business intending to grow, either combines with or buys out another firm with a view to create a new entity that can better leverage the joint strengths of both companies in the marketplace.

Maitre d'hôtel/Maitre d': Meaning 'Master of the House' in French, is in charge of allocating guests their tables and servers their dining areas each day. Being responsible for the overall dining experience and complaints if any, this person often plays the role of a de-facto restaurant manager and is thus considered to be key to a restaurant's success.

Mark up: An amount added to the cost price of a particular item to arrive at its selling price. This amount includes overheads and profit.

Menu: A menu is a statement of food and beverage items on offer, designed on the basis of guest needs and organizational objectives. This French word implies 'particulars'. Anecdotally, it originated in 1541 when Duke Henry of Brunswick was seen referring to a long slip of paper that reflected the list of dishes to be served. This enabled him to reserve his appetite accordingly.

Menu engineering: Identifying the most and the least popular and profitable dishes on the menu, with a view to eliminating or altering existing dishes and adding new ones, while considering their price and portion sizes.

Menu mix: The ratio of each item on the menu in relation to the rest of the items on the menu in terms of its sales, popularity and profit.

MEP: Mechanical, Electrical, and Plumbing designs that the architectural team develop, such as air-conditioning, ventilation, plumbing, fire protection systems, telecommunication systems, power and lighting, etc.

Michelin Star restaurant: Michelin, a French tire company launched its first guide book in 1900 to encourage road tripping, by anonymously reviewing restaurants for their culinary excellence. Inspectors across the world rate food at restaurants based on quality of products, mastery of technique, mastery of flavours, personality of cuisine and level of creativity, value for money, and consistency of food throughout the menu and through the year.

One Star: A very good restaurant in its category, offering cuisine prepared to a consistently high standard. A good place to stop on your journey.

Two Star: Excellent cuisine in its category, skilfully crafted dishes with specialities and wines of first class quality. Worth a detour.

Three Star: Exceptional cuisine, distinctive dishes, precisely executed using superlative ingredients. Often extremely expensive with outstanding wines. Worth a special journey.

A Bib Gourmand Award signifies quality food at a value price. Most other Michelin Star restaurants tend to be expensive.

Microbrewery: A space sometimes attached to a restaurant, where high quality flavoured craft beer is produced in small batches and sold fresh, usually without the addition of preservatives.

Minimum guaranteed: May refer to (a) Minimum Guaranteed Guests (Party Catering)–The minimum number of guests assured by the host as chargeable by the restaurant for a particular event, or (b) Minimum Guaranteed Rent–The minimum amount of rent assured to the landlord payable by the restaurant as a base figure, over and above which the landlord may be entitled to a percentage of the restaurant's sale (usually net of taxes).

Minimum wage: The lowest wage that an entrepreneur is permitted to pay by law, as per the employee's specific category (un-skilled, semi-skilled, skilled worker). The government defines minimum wage amounts to ensure that a basic standard of living by way of good health, comfort, dignity, education and contingencies are provided for its citizens.

MIS: Management Information Systems. Systems that capture the essence of management controls through concise formats.

Mise en place: Literally translated 'put in place'. In the cooking area, it refers to preparation of the kitchen for cooking by processing ingredients as well as keeping utensils and service-ware ready. In the dining area, it refers to preparation of the restaurant for service by table setting, serviceware cleaning, as well as sideboard stacking.

Mise en scene: Literally translated 'put in scene'. This refers to the broader picture in area preparation. It includes mise en place as well as general layout readiness.

Mixer (appliance):   A device used to mix foods or beverages in a kitchen or bar. Mixers may be either manual or electrical.

Mixer (drink):   Non-alcoholic beverages such as juices, sodas, etc., that are mixed with alcoholic beverages to create cocktails.

Mixology: The science and art of preparing mixed drinks.

Molecular gastronomy: A discipline of food science where chefs utilise their culinary knowledge with an understanding of physics and chemistry to innovatively and artistically transform the tastes and textures of foods. This experimental style of cooking uses some specialized ingredients, tools and techniques, including pressure, temperature and food chemical mixtures to create some extraordinary results, which include spheres, vapours, foams, and seemingly limitless other possibilities. Some refer to it as 'deconstructivist' or modernist cuisine.

Mood board: A collection of images, texts, and object samples that represents the proposed mood or feeling of a particular brand of restaurant or other retail space. Designers use it to visually illustrate the style they intend treating a certain space with, gathering feedback of others in the team, and gaining their concurrence.

MTD: Month to Date is the period starting at the beginning of the current month and ending at the current day. It is often used to see how the business is actually faring up to the current day versus its budget for that period in terms of sales, profits, etc.

Mystery dining: An exercise in which a restaurateur hires the services of a professional to visit the restaurant secretly and report on the delivery of the restaurant's brand experience in relation to its brand promise.

Napery: In a collective reference to restaurant linen fabric, including table cloths, runners, skirting of banquet-tables, napkins, aprons, etc.

NCNS: A 'No Call No Show' by an employee who goes on an unauthorized absence from work without notifying his employer. When this happens often or for a significant duration, a legal notice usually needs to be given and disciplinary action taken.

NDA: A Non-Disclosure Agreement is a legal contract between two or more parties restricting them from sharing confidential or proprietary information shared between them with any other party.

Neighbourhood considerations: Refers to sensitivity towards the residents of the neighbourhood in terms of disturbances such as sound, light, smoke, parking, religious and other sentiments.

(Net) Working Capital: Short-term assets (Cash + Accounts receivable + Inventory) less short-term liabilities (Accounts payable + Wages payable + Taxes payable).

No show: Either a guest who doesn't show up after making a table reservation or an employee who doesn't show up at work.

Nuke it: Microwave a dish, or an item required to prepare a dish.

ODC/OPC: Outdoor Catering/Outdoor Party Catering includes various social events from weddings to seminars, anniversaries to picnics that are catered to outdoors. While outdoor usually indicates open air spaces, it may also include enclosed spaces such as banquet halls where the caterer creates a temporary kitchen at the venue where he serves his guests.

Opex: Operating Expenditure is the ongoing cost of running a business, including the cost of materials, labour, and overheads.

Organic growth: Core internal growth of a company by increasing its output through expansion of its existing customer base and also by introducing new products or services.

Organoleptic tests: A sensory evaluation of food and beverages in areas, including product colour, appearance, hand-feel, mouth-feel, pliability, aroma, taste, etc., usually conducted by a trained professional or panel of judges.

OS&E: Operating Supplies and Equipment. Smallwares, including cutlery, crockery, glassware, linen, silverware, bar tools, kitchen tools, disposables, etc.

Outlay: The expenditure proposed to be incurred on a particular project or part thereof.

Outsourcing: Contracting some products or services to a third party so as to focus on its core competency, improve efficiency, save costs, etc. In the restaurant context for instance, services such as valet, housekeeping, dessert preparation, etc., are sometimes outsourced.

PAT: Profit After Tax

Pathogen: Bacteria, virus, fungi, etc., that may be disease causing or toxic.

Pax: A hospitality industry term used interchangeably with 'people'. So, number of pax is typically in reference to the number of guests at a restaurant, number of customers at a party, number of occupants in a hotel, number of passengers in an aircraft, etc.

PBT: Profit Before Tax

PDR: A Private Dining Room is a space separate from the main dining area of a restaurant where exclusive small gatherings may be hosted.

Performance appraisal: A systematic and periodic review and evaluation of an employee's work performance as against the goals outlined for him in his existing role by his superiors. The criteria of assessment may include job knowledge, productivity, initiative, adaptability, leadership ability, etc.

Pest: A creature capable of directly or indirectly contaminating food, that is therefore detrimental to human health.

Pick-up counter: A counter in the kitchen from which servers pick-up food items to be served to guests. One member of the kitchen staff barks out the order for each table and as each item is prepared, the kitchen staff deposit it on this table in readiness for a 'pick-up' by the servers.

Plating: Presenting food attractively on a plate, platter, or bowl to increase its appeal to restaurant guests is an art called plating. It involves highlighting the key ingredient with support ingredients while maintaining a balance of colours, textures, shapes, temperatures, and nutritional aspects. A white plate is considered by most as the best background to present their food's natural colours. Some find it aesthetically better to plate an odd number of pieces rather than even on their plate. Many chefs visualize a clock and have their favourite placement locations for each aspect of the meal corresponding to the hour, for example: protein between nine and eleven o'clock, starch between four and eight o'clock, vegetables between one and three o'clock.

Points/Point system: Refers to the allocation of predefined units for various levels of staff with an intention of equitable distribution of tips.

POP: Point of Purchase is a type of marketing material placed at locations where purchase decisions are made. For instance, a tall menu tent card displayed at a restaurant entrance or danglers hung above a food deli display counter.

Pop-up restaurant: A temporary restaurant where a chef can test-launch his food or a restaurateur can test-launch his concept in a brick and mortar format for just a few days or weeks with a live audience. Also called supper clubs, these restaurants can operate from a home, an existing restaurant during its non-peak hours, an event centre, a gallery, a factory, or even a vehicle, thereby limiting the capital expenditure and the licensing requirements. Patrons are usually informed of pop-up restaurants through social media, and often appreciate their creativity, variety, and affordability.

Portion control: The establishment of standards in a restaurant for the weight, size, and number of items in each dish that the organization will serve consistently regardless of when or by whom.

POS: Point of Sale is the location at which sales transactions occur. While in a restaurant this happens between the guest and the server at the table, the computer terminals referred to as POS terminals, capture sales transactions and print receipts at sideboards nearby.

PR: Public Relations. Endeavours made by the entrepreneur to give a social image to his establishment.

Prepping: The act of preparing the kitchen and dining area of the restaurant for guests in the upcoming shift.

Private equity: Money invested in companies that haven't gone public, i.e., those that are not listed on the stock exchange.

Product Mix: The full range of products on offer (on the menu).

Proof of concept: Evidence that demonstrates the feasibility of a particular business model or concept, wins the confidence of its investors. For instance, an entrepreneur who with his existing restaurant can show proof of success in terms of consumer demand, return on investment, profitability, operational efficiency, solidity in team, etc., is more likely to be funded to scale up his brand to multiple locations.

Push it: Sell it. A dish may need to be hard-sold at times when it is nearing the end of its shelf life or when money might be lost by not selling the dish immediately.

QSR: Restaurants that were earlier referred to as Fast Food Restaurants are now called Quick Service Restaurants.

Quick and dirty: A task where speed and convenience are more important than quality.

R&D: Research and Development of new products, services or processes that can better fulfil market needs.

Ramekin: Fireproof dishes in which individual portions of savoury or dessert items are both baked and served. A Ramekin is also the name of a food made of cheese, egg, and breadcrumbs prepared within a Ramekin dish.

Ramen profitable: A business that is making just about enough money for its promoters to make ends meet. This buys some time for the business to continue surviving in the marketplace. Being Ramen Profitable is not just good for the morale of the entrepreneur, but also improves the promoter's relationship with his investors.

Regulars: Guests who patronize a business frequently enough to be rewarded, or at least more personally acknowledged than other guests. Repeat patrons are a critical factor in the success of a restaurant businesses.

Reserves: A company's assets kept readily available as cash or investments.

Rest room/Area: Space allocated for staff relaxation, changing of attire, and grooming.

Restaurateur: The manager or owner of a restaurant.

RevPAR: Revenue Per Available Room is a measure of the financial performance or health of a hotel. It is a function of room rates (per night) and occupancy.

RevPAR = Total Net Room Revenue[†]/Number of available rooms in the same period

[†] net of discounts and taxes, and not including revenue from meals.

RevPASH: Revenue Per Available Seat Hour is a measure of the financial performance or health of a restaurant. It is a function of seat revenue (per hour) and occupancy.

RevPASH = Total Net Food and Beverage Revenue[†] / Number of available seats in the same period

[†] net of discounts and taxes.

Right of first refusal: A contractual right within a business agreement, that allows one party the privilege of first exercising or rejecting an option granted by the other party. For instance, a landlord may grant his tenant the first right of refusal in extending their agreement beyond the initially proposed period. Only if the tenant declines, can the landlord put his property up for rent to an alternate tenant.

Robot-coupe: A commercial food preparation equipment manufacturer head-quartered in France. It is most renowned for its reliable, heavy duty food processors through industry kitchens across the world.

ROI: Return on Investment, is a measure of business performance that evaluates the efficiency of gains from a particular investment.

Roll-up: Silverware wrapped in a napkin which may be either linen or paper.

Roux: Pronounced 'Roo', this is a mixture of equal parts of melted fat (butter or vegetable oil or lard) and flour, cooked together as the base for the three mother sauces of French classical cooking (béchamel, velouté, and espagnole). Roux is also used as a thickener for soups, stews, and gravies. The extent to which the roux is cooked contributes to the flavour and colour of the final dish.

Runner: A food runner is a busboy/busser. A table runner is a table accessory made of narrow fabric or paper used to drape a table at a restaurant.

Running order/On the fly: Refers to an order that needs to be served right away. This is either because the guest is getting late, the rest of the guests at the table have been served, a guest needs to leave urgently, a dish is inedible, or because the waiter has delayed or made a mistake with an order that needs to be replaced or served urgently.

Russian Service: Food pre-cooked and pre-portioned in the kitchen is brought to the table on platters and served quickly and with formality from the left of a guest, usually at banquet functions.

Salamander: An electric or gas powered oven with high temperature overhead heating elements used to grill sandwiches, melt cheese, brown baked dishes, etc.

Same-store sales: A metric that measures growth in restaurants or retail stores that have been doing business for more than 12 months. From the 13th month onwards, the revenue and growth of the restaurant can be compared to its own performance in the same period the previous year. This can be done for a particular week, month or financial quarter the previous year, and once the second year of being in business is complete, you could compare the entire year's sales to the previous year's sales.

Sangria: Spanish drink made from sweet red wine, pieces of fresh fruit like orange, lemon, etc., and spices like cinnamon, cloves, etc.

Sanitizing: Cleaning or disinfecting surfaces that are prone to harbouring bacteria and compromising the health or safety of restaurant guests.

SBU: Strategic Business Units are autonomous operational divisions within large companies that have independent missions and objectives. They are small enough to respond quickly to market situations, but large enough to control most factors influencing their long term performance.

SCM: Supply Chain Management covers the management of inventory (either stored or in transit) — right from the raw material stage at the vendor's premises until the point of consumption and includes all the various work-in-progress stages in between. In the case of food, it involves the management of inventory from farm to plate.

SEC: Socio Economic Classification is the way marketers categorize their potential customers on the basis of occupation and education of the chief wage earner of a household in India. This is based on a flawed assumption that higher education always leads to higher income and therefore higher consumption potential. For instance, a post graduate executive may be likely to have a higher income and therefore higher consumption potential, but a trader or retailer with almost no education may be earning and consuming more.

Server (computer):   Main computer that stores consolidated data accessed by other computers or POS units on the network.

Server (person):   A waiter or waitress serving the guest.

Service charge: An additional charge for a service for which there is already a basic fee. At a restaurant, it may involve adding an additional percentage of the bill to the total bill, often in lieu of tipping.

Sharking/Poaching (employees): When an entrepreneur or a business head from one restaurant, persuades an employee from a competing restaurant, to join them instead. Fellow restaurateurs often-times call for a truce on poaching so as not to hurt one another's businesses.

Sharking/Poaching (tables): When a server intercepts guests being led to other tables and redirects them to his own tables for his own benefit.

Shelf life: The amount of time for which a food or other perishable item may be kept on the shelf or served to a guest, without becoming unsuitable for consumption or unsuitable for cooking. A fresh-cream cake for example, may have a "best consumed by" number of hours on the label, after which its freshness may begin to deteriorate.

Shorting: Like short-changing, a cashier may be shorting a restaurant of money, a vendor may be shorting a restaurant of wares, or a guest shorting a restaurant of money due to the restaurant by way of the check.

Sideboard/Station: A pre-service setup area in the dining room containing extra cutlery, crockery, glassware, linen, accompaniments, water jugs, hot plates, POS system, etc.

Signature dish: A recipe that epitomises the distinctive style of cooking of a particular restaurant or a particular chef by which that restaurant or chef may be identified.

Silver service: A formal style of service wherein food is transferred from a service dish to the guest's plate from his left using a service spoon and fork. Clearing of plates and serving of beverages is done from the guest's right. Further, guests seated at the table are served clockwise, ladies first followed by the gentlemen and lastly the host.

SLA: Service Level Agreement is a contract between two parties that represents the minimum performance criteria that a service provider promises to deliver to its customer. It usually comprises of service provider deliverables, including basic measurable service level scheduled, problem handling, response time, warranties, penalties payable against gaps in delivery, etc., as well as customer responsibilities.

Smorgasbord: Swedish for Open-faced Sandwich table, this term refers loosely to a buffet of hors d'oeuvres, smoked and pickled fish, hot and cold meats, cheeses, salads, and relishes.

Soft launch: A method of announcing the opening of a restaurant to a limited audience with little fanfare. The intent is to first get their buy-in, before making it available to the general public.

Sommelier: A French term for a wine steward who has expertise in wine varieties, their procurement, storage, and service. In high-end restaurants that offer such wine, a sommelier will help the restaurant select its wines, work in conjunction with the chef to plan the pairing of wines with food, and accordingly recommend suitable options to guests, as per their tastes and budgets.

SOP: Standard Operating Procedures are a set of operational instructions (usually in the form of a manual) with a view to ensure uniformity in the maintenance of predetermined standards of performance and delivery of guest experience.

Sous chef: Literally meaning Under Chef, the number two person after the executive chef or head chef, in charge of the kitchen.

Speed pourer: A device fitted at the mouth of a bottle (usually liquor) to facilitate a speedy flow and accurate quantity of the drink without spillage. Particularly useful during peak hours at a bar, the bartender's practised hand times each pour to perfection sometimes sliding his thumb or finger over the air-hole to control the pour.

Speed rail: A bottle holder usually made of stainless steel in easy reach of the bartender to facilitate speedy service to guests. Based on the bar menu, the bartender keeps within it the most often used bottles of spirits, other liquors, and mixers.

Stand-alone restaurant: One that is independent of supporting infrastructure such as may be available within a hotel. For example: stores, administrative offices, housekeeping, etc.

Store-in-Store: The location of a restaurant situated within another business such as a mall, theatre, casino, airport, railway station, etc., where the existing patrons of the larger business are tapped as potential patrons of the restaurant. The success or failure of the larger business often influences the destiny of the restaurant and so restaurateurs sometimes try and sign up for such a location with an entrance independent of the mall.

Succession planning: The identification and development of internal talent to meet the future goals of the company. It prepares people for leadership roles in readiness to take charge when the need arises.

Sunny side up: A style of fried egg with only one side cooked, thereby leaving the yolk on top intact like a sun.

Sweat equity: A shareholding in a company earned by an individual's effort rather than money invested by him in a partnership. In a start-up, apart from co-founding partners who may hold shares by virtue of their "sweat", some employees may also be offered stock equity alongside a basic salary which is usually lower than a salary that equals their market value.

TA/TM: Target Audience/Target Market are specific groups of customers that are targeted as your ideal guests in a start-up or your preferred guests in an existing restaurant business based on characteristics such as age, gender, income, education, buying habits, etc.

Table d'hôte: A fixed menu prepared in advance, offering limited options at a set price and time.

Table turns: The number of sittings per meal at each table through the opening hours of the restaurant are known as table turns. To ensure and improve profit in the restaurant business, table turns need to be done, though without the guests feeling rushed. For instance, a fine dining restaurant can have two table turns at dinner while a casual dining restaurant with a shorter guest dining time may do three or more table turns.

Tableware: All table appointments in a restaurant, including cutlery, crockery, glassware, linen, cruet set, bud-vase, ashtray, etc.

Tasting menu: An array of dishes served in small portions, specially chosen by the chef as a showcase of the restaurants best offerings.

The floor: Getting on to the floor means getting out of a place of low activity like an office for instance, to an area where the action is! While this mostly refers to areas where the customers are, it is also used in context with back of the house areas of action like the kitchen.

Tips/Gratuity: Money left by the guest in exchange for a service performed.

Top line: The top item of a profit and loss statement, which could variously be the Revenue, Sales, Turnover or Income.

TTL: 'Through the line' refers to those sales and marketing techniques which integrate both the ATL and the BTL promotional methods.

Udupi: A little town in Karnataka, India, whose local cuisine was originally cooked at the Krishna Matt Temple in Udupi. Their quick, clean, and economical vegetarian meals, slowly made their way into the hearts of many people in different parts of the country. Starting with their own cuisine including idlis and dosas, they went on to create and offer their own versions of Chinese food and also pizza which are quite popular amongst Indians the world over. In the restaurant business, Udupi restaurants are admired for their resourcefulness and innovation.

Upselling: A sales technique that involves the server exposing the customer to options that are more expensive or more profitable for the establishment.

UPS: Uninterruptible Power Supply is a device that provides energy backup to the IT system during electricity fluctuation or failure, thereby enabling the user to save valuable data.

Upside sharing: Sharing the 'upside' with the landlord of a restaurant would mean that in a situation where sales exceeds expectations projected by the restaurateur, he would be willing to share a percentage of those increased sales with his landlord thereby putting both sides in a win-win situation.

USP: Unique Selling Proposition. The distinctive factor that differentiates a product or service from competitors.

Valuation: Determining the worth of a company by analyzing the market value of its assets, its future prospective earnings, the composition of its capital structure, and the quality of the company's management. Valuation of a company is required during a merger or acquisition, tax assessments, business analysis, etc.

VAT: Value Added Tax is a consumption tax levied at each stage of the production or distribution of a product based on the value added to the product at that stage.

Venture Capital: Money provided to a company in its early stages in return for a share in equity. Though such investment may be considered high risk, high reward, investors with sound business acumen are usually able to identify high-potential businesses that are scalable. Usually, venture capitalists invest after the proof of concept stage.

VFM: Value for Money. The fair amount a consumer perceives a particular product or service to be worth.

Volume discount: When purchasing a large quantity of some supplies, a vendor may be willing to give you a better price.

Waitlist: A list of guests waiting to be seated at a restaurant while it is full. The restaurant representative handling the seating writes down the name of the host of each group in the order they arrive along with the number of their guests. Then as the occupied tables clear up, she allocates a table based on a first-come first-served basis and a match between table size and group size based on the policy of the restaurant. While a celebrity skipping this line rarely goes down well with other waiting guests, a handicapped person skipping it is often more acceptable.

Walk-in (cooler/freezer): A refrigerated storage room for food and beverage within which a person can actual walk-in and collect his requirements.

Walk-in (guest): A guest who directly walks into the restaurant without a prior reservation.

YTD: Year-to-date is the period starting at the beginning of the current year and ending at the current day. It is often used to see how the business is actually faring up to the current day versus its budget for that period in terms of sales, profits, etc.

A Few Culinary Terms

Allspice/Jamaica Pepper: The dried, unripe berry of a small tree used in seed or powder form to season casseroles, cakes, and puddings.

Arborio rice: Starchy, short-grained, Italian rice used in the preparation of risotto.

Aubergine: The 'long purple' of Indian origin also known as eggplant or brinjal.

Au Gratin: Dish covered with sauce, cheese or breadcrumbs, then baked/grilled and served in the dish in which it was cooked.

Baking powder: Baking soda (Soda Bicarbonate) + Cream of Tartar.

Balsamic vinegar: Dark and pungently sweet Italian vinegar made from white Trebbiano grapes. Used in salad dressing and marinades.

Bisque: A thick, rich, cream soup made from shellfish.

Calamari: Squid served as a Mediterranean speciality.

Canapés: Well-garnished open faced sandwiches with a savoury topping, using a base of toast, fried bread, pastry, etc.

Cilantro: The leaf of the coriander plant also known as Chinese, Thai, or Mexican parsley.

Couscous: Nutty-flavoured rice substitute with origins in North Africa. The grain of the wheat plant that may be dried or milled for pasta making.

Cream of tartar: A potassium salt of tartaric acid extracted from grape juice. Used in baking powder to leaven batter (combines with baking soda to produce carbon dioxide in the presence of moisture, and optionally heat).

Crêpe: A thin often translucent pancake stuffed with sweet or savoury fillings.

Croûtons: Small pieces of bread usually cubed and then either toasted or fried till crisp. Used with soups, salads, and appetizers.

Dim Sum: Broadly refers to a selection of small dishes served as snacks or a meal in China. Usually in reference to steamed or fried dumplings.

Escalopes: Thin slices of meat dipped in egg and breadcrumbs and then fried.

Five spice: A combination of powdered Chinese spices, including star anise, cinnamon, clove, pepper, and fennel.

Focaccia: An Italian flatbread made with pizza or bread dough, baked plain, or, with toppings like onions, tomatoes, zucchini, eggplant, etc.

Mascarpone: A soft and creamy Italian cheese used in the making of Tiramisu.

MSG: Monosodium Glutamate is a sodium salt used to intensify the natural flavour of certain foods. It is an important ingredient in Chinese and Japanese cuisines. MSG elicits a unique taste, known as 'umami', that is different from the four basic tastes (bitter, salty, sour, sweet). It enhances the complex flavours of meat, poultry, seafood, and vegetables, and is used in many canned, frozen, and packaged foods. MSG has been controversial since reports of an allergic reaction in some individuals.

Okra: Lady's finger.

Pastrami: Seasoned smoked beef.

Pawpaw: Papaya.

Polenta: Cornmeal used to make a thick porridge.

Shiitake: Fleshy black Chinese forest mushrooms that have a woody flavour.

Sweetbreads: Savoury delicacies made from the innards (thymus, heart, stomach, pancreas, gullet) of young calves and lambs.

Sweetmeats: Small, shaped pieces of confectionery.

Tahini: Thick paste made from sesame seeds used in Middle Eastern cooking.

Truffle: Subterranean fungus valued as a delicacy in France, gathered by specially trained pigs or dogs.

Wasabi: Japanese horseradish paste served as a condiment with sushi.

Zucchini/Courgette: Cucumber-like, long green vegetable.

Methods of Cooking

Baking: Cooking food in an enclosed space (oven). The food itself may release some steam during the process. For e.g., cakes, bread, vegetables, etc.

Boiling: This involves the movement of liquid using heat to encourage vaporisation. The food to be cooked must be surrounded by the boiling liquid. The boiling point can differ based on altitude or use of a pressure cooker.

Braising: First browning the meat or vegetable in a little fat, then immersing it to half to two-thirds its depth in liquid, and finally simmering till tender in a tightly-sealed pot.

Broiling: Cooking food using a direct heat source–synonymous with grilling.

Frying: Bringing the food in contact with hot oil or fat so as to seal and brown it. The food may sometimes be covered with flour, breadcrumbs or batter.

Grilling/Roasting: The food is cooked by direct contact with dry heat (usually on a metal grid or a tray) using coal, gas, or electricity. Roasting is generally used for thick meats rather than poultry and supported by frequent basting with dripping from the roast.

Poaching: The food is cooked by simmering in water or other liquids. The liquid should never be boiled and is later discarded. Used for egg, fish, fruit, etc. To retain the shape and appearance of eggs to be poached you may use a poaching pan or mild vinegar.

Sautéing: The food is tossed in a shallow pan with a little fat for a short duration.

Sous Vide: Literally meaning 'Under Vacuum', this is a cooking method where foods like meat, fish, etc., are vacuum packed in a plastic pouch or glass jar immersed in a warm water bath at low temperatures and cooked for many hours.

Steaming: Surrounding the food in the steam of fast boiling water. This is a slow process as the food is placed in a tray or other dish within the one in which the water is boiling.

Dining Etiquette

It is interesting to take a look at a few of the unfathomable dining graces that are considered socially useful in creating a favourable professional or personal impression.

Reservations: Prior table booking with a mention of special occasion or preferred seating is advised.

Seating: Gentlemen should seat the ladies if the server has not already taken care of it.

Posture: Sit upright with your arms near your body. You may lightly place your elbows on the side of the table while leaning forward, but heavily placing them on the table is improper.

Napkin: Once seated, napkins may be placed on your lap right away. When leaving the table, it may be placed thereon without refolding.

Beginning: Wait till everyone is served to begin eating. Since the food may become cold, it's also all right to start if others indicate you may commence without them.

Soup: Circle the spoonful of soup away from the bowl before bringing it to your mouth rather than directly to your mouth. You may tilt the bowl away from your body for the last few spoonfuls.

Passing the salt: Place the salt-pepper shaker, bread, etc., on the table within reach of the guest rather than directly in someone's hand. If the items are not within your reach, ask the other person to pass them to you rather than reaching out yourself.

Portioning: Serve yourself/others a little bit of everything. Decline dishes not to your liking politely. Eat small mouthfuls at a time at the pace of the other diners.

Finger foods: It is acceptable to use your fingers with items like chips, appetizers, cookies, small fruit, sandwiches, bread, etc.

Selection: It is desirable to develop a working knowledge of food, wine, serviceware, and cigars to help make a selection.

Eating style: European: Fork in left hand, tines pointed downward to facilitate food grip. Knife in right hand to cut mouth size pieces. To eat, move left hand to the mouth with tines pointing downward.

American: Cut pieces same as above. To eat, place knife on plate and shift fork to right hand with tines pointing upward.

Removing inedible morsels: While removing inedible morsels from your mouth you must be discrete so as not to offend your fellow diners. You may place the article in the spoon or fork that carried it to your mouth or even the pit of your hand. While extracting an embedded piece of food with a toothpick, your free hand should cover your mouth.

Conversing: If asked something while chewing, smile close mouthed, and reply after swallowing your food.

Excusing yourself: You may excuse yourself to answer nature's call or if you are feeling unwell.

Put offs: Smoking, answering your phone, and objectionable food-related noises.

Dropped articles: If you accidentally drop an item of cutlery or a napkin within your reach, you may reach out for it yourself and request that it be replaced. If it is not within a 'dignified' reach you may signal the server to pick it up for you.

On completion: When you have finished your meal, do not push your plate away. You may indicate the same to your server by placing the knife and fork alongside each other either in the 12-6 o'clock position or the 10-4 o'clock diagonal.

Paying the check: Signal the server for the check and settle the bill. If you are not the host you may offer to help paying. If the host declines, let it go and thank him for the meal.

Acknowledgements

I owe my knowledge to the many brilliant minds of the entrepreneurs and colleagues with whom I have had the privilege of working and sharing experiences.

I gratefully acknowledge the suggestions and editorial contributions made by my wife Seema, my friend Dr. AVS Prasad, and most importantly, by my brother Chirag, without whom this project would never have been brought to a successful conclusion.

A special thanks to my publisher Akash and the rest of the Jaico team for their well-balanced approach and patience in making this journey a friction-free and enjoyable one.

The first hard-copy version of this book titled Showtime was published by English Edition in 2005. This is a significantly revised edition. Please feel free to send me your suggestions and comments at raviwazir@gmail.com

About the Author

Ravi Wazir, a seasoned strategist with over three decades of experience, has spearheaded the growth of SMEs, MNCs, and family-run enterprises across India. A graduate of Institute of Hotel Management, Mumbai, and an SME programme alum of IIM-Ahmedabad, he's played pivotal roles at Olive, Izumi, Swati Snacks, and many other top restaurants. He also ran his own executive meal enterprise.

A notable contributor to Forbes India and DNA Money, Ravi is a distinguished speaker at forums like The Indian Chamber of Commerce and IIM-A. Currently, he channels his expertise into consulting and leadership interventions for entrepreneurs.

Ravi was born and raised in Bandra, Mumbai where he presently lives with his wife and two kids.

JAICO PUBLISHING HOUSE

Elevate Your Life. Transform Your World.

ESTABLISHED IN 1946, Jaico Publishing House is home to world-transforming authors such as Sri Sri Paramahansa Yogananda, Osho, the Dalai Lama, Sri Sri Ravi Shankar, Sadhguru, Robin Sharma, Deepak Chopra, Jack Canfield, Eknath Easwaran, Devdutt Pattanaik, Khushwant Singh, John Maxwell, Brian Tracy, and Stephen Hawking.

Our late founder Mr. Jaman Shah first established Jaico as a book distribution company. Sensing that independence was around the corner, he aptly named his company Jaico ('Jai' means victory in Hindi). In order to service the significant demand for affordable books in a developing nation, Mr. Shah initiated Jaico's own publications. Jaico was India's first publisher of paperback books in the English language.

While self-help, religion and philosophy, mind/body/spirit, and business titles form the cornerstone of our non-fiction list, we publish an exciting range of travel, current affairs, biography, and popular science books as well. Our renewed focus on popular fiction is evident in our new titles by a host of fresh young talent from India and abroad. Jaico's recently established translations division translates selected English content into nine regional languages.

Jaico distributes its own titles. With its headquarters in Mumbai, Jaico has branches in Ahmedabad, Bangalore, Chennai, Delhi, Hyderabad, and Kolkata.

SINCE 1946